THE CONVERGENCE OF MACHINE AND HUMAN NATURE

The Convergence of Machine and Human Nature

A critique of the computer metaphor of mind and artificial intelligence

ALEXANDER McCLINTOCK

Avebury

Aldershot · Brookfield USA · Hong Kong · Singapore · Sydney

Published by
Avebury
Ashgate Publishing Ltd
Gower House
Croft Road
Aldershot
Hants. GU11 3HR
England

Ashgate Publishing Company
Old Post Road
Brookfield
Vermont 05036
USA

British Library Cataloguing in Publication Data

McClintock, Alexander
  Convergence of Machine and Human Nature:
  Critique of the Computer Metaphor of
  Mind and Artificial Intelligence. -
  (Avebury Series in Philosophy)
  I. Title II. Series
  006.301

ISBN 1 85628 997 4

Library of Congress Catalog Card Number: 94-79818

Printed in Great Britain by Ipswich Book Co. Ltd., Ipswich,

Contents

Acknowledgments

I would like to thank, David Cockburn and Rocky Rockingham-Gill for their encouragment, wisdom and teaching, and Kathrin Haase for her support.

Introduction

The idea that a person might be created by any means other than 'the begetting of a child on a woman by a man' has long been thought of as horrific or evil. It has also exercised some fascination on peoples minds: In various persecutions, witches were sometimes accused of creating children by magical means, - these allegedly had no navel, - and Goethe[1] has the character Wagner alchemically create a 'homonculus' or 'manikin' which is a cousin to Mephistophles. To usurp the natural process of creating life is almost always seen as evil. Recently, reports that geneticists are analysing or making living things with the basic materials of life have sparked emotive commentaries in the mass media about scientists 'playing God'.

Yet beside this may be set the common prejudices that mechanism is true, the world (including humans) consists entirely of matter, and that, given time and resources, technology will be able to create anything that can be described clearly. It can easily appear that one day we will be able to build a person as we might build a new machine.

The recent successes of computer science have led some people[2] to claim just that. Most authors in the field are much more cautious and are aware of some of the problems that arise from prejudices in favour of mechanism, materialism, and the future triumphs of technology. Such plausibility as the claim that it will one day be possible to build an artificial person may have derives largely from the apparent success of the computational metaphor in explaining some aspects of mind and human psychology.

Some cognitive psychologists want to draw a distinction between the 'computational metaphor', and the 'computational view of thought'. The basis of the distinction is that the computational view of thought does not claim that an electronic computer is a physical model for thought. It does however understand thinking as involving representations which:

> must be expressed in some internal language containing

1

definitions for well-formed structures and operations upon them [Hunt Earl, 1989, vol. 40, pp. 603-626].

Since my criticisms are aimed at any view of mind which explains its functioning in terms of representations and processes which are even similar to those of a computer I expect that my criticisms will have the same force against the computational view of mind as against the computer metaphor. Hunt[3] quotes Fodor, whom I criticise below, as an authority.

The grounds for the belief in the possibility of building an artificial person is the perceived explanatory power of the computer metaphor. In this essay I want to challenge on conceptual grounds two of the hypotheses of the computer metaphor. The first is that the mind contains representations, the second is that mentation or cognition is best understood as a process. I shall then go on to sketch some of the things that I believe, for conceptual reasons, must be true of anything that can correctly be called a person. I hope to show that these things make it formidably difficult, if not impossible, for the computer metaphor to provide a route to person building. In the process of doing so I believe that I will demonstrate that the computer metaphor is of limited use for understanding mind and that our concept of 'person' is very closely connected to the human form.

Notes

1.   Goethe, J. W. (1949), Wayne Philip (Trans.), *Faust Part 2, Act 2,* Penguin Books, London

2.   Simons, Geoff. (1983), *Are Computers Alive: Evolution and New Life forms* Harvester Press, Brighton,
        also
        Pollock, John. L. (1989), *How To Build A Person: A Prologomenon* M.I.T. Press, Cambridge Mass

3.   Hunt, Earl (1989), Cognitive Science, Definitions, Status, and Questions', *Annual Review of Psychology*, vol. 40, p.604.

1 Philosophical attitudes and artificial intelligence

People who work in research in Artificial Intelligence tend to think of themselves as scientists and of their subject as having affinities with empirical psychology and with engineering. In conceiving of themselves in this way they naturally take the attitudes of scientists and engineers. Theories are said to be no more than tentative hypotheses to be tested against empirical psychology. Their hope (or fear), is that if they work long enough and hard enough in the same way as they are doing now they will unlock the fundamental secrets of mind. In short, there appears to be an unspoken faith in the ultimate success of endeavours modelled on the paradigm sciences, such as physics and chemistry, to give satisfying answers to all our questions about mind.

This faith seems to me to determine in advance what kinds of conclusion researchers in A.I. may draw about mind: To approach the problems of mind from such an intellectual environment is to approach these problems bearing those philosophical attitudes that have made modern theories of matter possible. These attitudes do not form part of some well articulated coherent theory in which modern scientific theories are grounded but rather are a mass of accretions from various philosophical theories which have played a role in the history of science and which, in their time, have served science well.

With such attitudes underlying a research programme into the nature of mind it is not surprising to find that the results produced and the conclusions reached have tended to drift towards a radical re-evaluation of our status as moral and spiritual beings. (It was this drift and its alarming implications that prompted Joseph Weisenbaum's book 'Computer Power and Human Reason'[1] which advocates a moral limitation to such research.)

One example of these philosophical attitudes which form the intellectual environment of modern science is the idea that matter, as studied by physicists, is inanimate. The significance of this is that it justifies an approach to the behaviour of the natural universe which may ignore any suggestion that the behaviour of bodies (such as the motion of planets, or the mutual repulsion, or attraction of magnets), is a consequence of their volitions or attitudes or any other attribute of mind. Motion of bodies, for physicists, is to be explained in terms of prior causes, universal laws, and innate properties of bodies.

This approach to matter was sanctioned by,[2] and has grown out of, Descartes' philosophical theory, which divided the universe into two ontological categories, namely, material substance and immaterial substance. Spirit and the activities of mind were confined in this theory to immaterial substance. For Descartes, material substance with soul (i.e. persons), was a special case which was not subject to the universal laws which governed the behaviour of material substance. Matter, the proper subject of the study of Physics, was material substance without soul and thus volitions and the like did not come into question. Affinities, repulsions and attractions between substances or bodies, bonding, and other predicates which find their paradigmatic application in human affairs had to be understood metaphorically when applied to matter.

This attitude has been imported into some disciplines which involve the study of persons with great success in some areas (for example medicine), however in such areas the successes which can clearly be seen to depend on this attitude, (e.g. prosthetics, surgery, dentistry, etc.) involve detailed study of parts of a person only.

In dividing the Universe into two parts in this way Descartes set himself an insoluble problem: The two substances could never interact because their non-interaction was, in effect, but not explicitly stated as such, one of their defining properties. This leads to all sorts of problems: For example, even if immaterial substance exists, a spirit could never know it was located in its body. Thus bodies could only 'have' spirits by remote chance (or continuous divine intervention). Descartes seems to have been aware of this problem and to have regarded it as soluble. He does not explain how it is to be solved, but simply maintains that there is interaction.

If in trying to solve this problem we reject ontological dualism we immediately create problems for anyone who would bring the traditional perspectives of modern physics to the study of human bodies and minds: It seems obvious that explanatory schema which may be appropriate to bodies like billiard balls are inappropriate to bodies which have volitions, intentions, and such like and are capable of saying so clearly, yet in an ontologically monist account of the world billiard balls and human bodies partake of the same most general schema of explanation.

This observation is not in itself fatal to any project to build an artificial

4

person. Indeed the kind of simplistic materialism that holds that intentions, volitions, thoughts, and other forms of mentation are all eliminatively reducible to physical and chemical terms has been argued against by philosophers (whom I shall criticise below), who believe in the future success of A.I., for example D.C. Dennett and H. Putnam. Part of what attracts Dennett to computational theories of mind is that it seems to him to provide a way of maintaining ontological monism while rejecting any kind of eliminative reduction of mentation to physical and chemical terms. This however does not undermine my point that the attitudes and activities of the sciences on which workers in the field of A.I. would model their activities carry with them neo-cartesian philosophical perspectives and habits of thought which are inappropriate for the study of mind when it is understood as grounded in matter.

The whole A.I. project and computer metaphor, in so far as it is conceived of as helping to provide a monist explanation of mind rather than as a branch of machine tool technology, is for this reason deeply flawed. The very idea that a clear understanding of mind could be gained from a project that models itself on physics or other of the hard sciences can be seen to arise out of incoherent thought, namely that if we make a sufficiently detailed study of objects which, by hypothesis, lack mind, we will thereby come to an understanding of mind. Thus the conclusions which workers in A.I. may arrive at as explanations of hopes, fears, loves, hates, moral values, visions, and so on are grounded in observations, studies, and sciences which presuppose that that which is to be explained (hopes etc.), is not a property of that which is being studied, (i.e. matter).

This state of affairs does not make the A.I. project pointless. For many researchers in the field, A.I. is about making better tools. Those who conceive of A.I. as having the building of persons as a long term goal might reasonably point out that science is not a formal logical system proceeding from one well-formed logical formula to the next by means of rules of inference, and that this is the most that is shown by my criticism. A little incoherence in science may well be tolerable, it might even be helpful, but this historical background should at least give A.I. enthusiasts pause for thought. Any conclusions arising from A.I. research which seem to point to a re-evaluation of the moral status or value of persons or qualities of mind must be regarded as suspect simply on account of their origin. At the very least they would need to be supported by reasoning which is not modelled on that of the paradigm sciences. More generally, a systematic attempt to create a modern, monist, account of persons would inspire more confidence in its conclusions if it could be shown that the historical foundations of its concepts lay in an account of the world which took mind to be present in some pieces of the world as a natural phenomenon (just as the hardness of rocks is a natural phenomenon). Aristotle's philosophy and some schools of neo-platonism would be candidates for this.

It seems that many authors are tacitly aware that there are problems of this kind and therefore proceed in the faith that, as science has a good history of providing satisfactory explanations, they may forge ahead with confidence and, having gained an understanding, come back to this problem at a later date. This seems to me to be subject to the criticism that any history of the successes of science may be countered by a history of the failures of science.

Having noted these reservations about the intellectual foundations of A.I. and any project to build an artificial person, I will move on to a critique of such projects as they appear in the writings of five of its more philosophical authors.

These projects are elaborations of descriptions of an operating computer as a metaphor of mind. The computational metaphor is nothing if it is not concerned with process. Computers are machines which manipulate symbols sequentially according to a pre-determined program.[3] Any computer which is operating is a machine executing a process.

Once one has accepted the thought that people might be a bit like computers and have analogous processes, it is a small step to thinking that there must be something which is processed (perhaps analogous to the data which a computer processes). In Artificial Intelligence this role is usually filled by the notion of representations', and data gathered directly from the environment. Representations are usually thought of as themselves having been built up from data supplied by or acquired from the environment. Representations are posited as theoretically necessary objects.[4] Without representations all that the hypothesised computer program may take as 'data' are environmental stimuli, and the only possible outcome of the processing of the 'data' is some form of mechanical response. By this I mean that the consequence of the process must be a change in the machine's 'body', such as the movement of an 'arm'. The consequence cannot be a change in the 'inner' representation of its environment, for in this case there is no such representation. Thus without representations the computer metaphor collapses into a primitive form of behaviourism.

The notion of representation has a number of attractions: First it fits into the computer metaphor quite nicely. Second, taken with the notion of process it appears to be a good candidate to explain what it is to have an inner life (e.g. a capacity to deliberate, hold a commitment, imagine a more beautiful world, etc). Third, it dovetails quite neatly with current psychological theories about learning and associated theories of cognitive psychology. In addition to all this, it appears to solve some long standing and acute problems in theories of language that make appeal to deep formal grammars underlying linguistic practice.

In chapter 3 of this essay I shall criticise the notions of 'representation' and 'process' as it appears in some of the literature relating to Artificial Intelligence and Cognitive Psychology. I shall note some of the areas of mentation where I think the description of what is going on as some kind of process must be false. I shall also be concerned to show that representations as they are usually understood within the computer metaphor cannot solve the problems of mind that they were invented to solve and are in any case unnecessary. In doing this I believe that I can show that the computer metaphor has explanatory power for at most a few restricted aspects of mind.

All proponents of the possibility of person building or strong 'A.I.' rest their optimism in some way on the computer metaphor. This includes those, like John Pollock, whose argument is based on an account of functionalism. The supposition, in his case, which is necessary to such a position, that the necessary 'bits' of machinery with the right functional attributes (according to the functional theory in question), could, in principle, be built, is grounded in Turing theory and its assurance that a machine can be built which instantiates any partially recursive function. Thus in showing that the computer metaphor is of very limited use in any attempt to understand mind more clearly, I believe I will have removed the only plausible ground that has been offered to date for the belief that an artificial person might one day be built.

In chapters 4 and 5 of this essay I shall suggest some properties that anything that is to be a candidate for personhood must have. These, if they are correct, impose restrictions on what kinds of things we might correctly describe as persons. In particular they exclude most types of machine that are presently contemplated as possible candidates for personhood.

Inevitably, given such a subject, there is a risk of philosophy sliding into 'arm-chair psychology'. My interest is principally in philosophical questions and not in psychological ones. That is to say that my interest in this essay is to criticise the concepts employed in the computer metaphor of mind and any light it may shed on questions such as 'What is mind?', and not in the relations between theories of perception,

7

learning, cognition, and such like, and physiology.

Notes

1. Weisenbaum, Joseph (1984), *Computer Power and Human Reason*, Penguin Books.

2. Naturally the observation that some objects such as stones do not have volitions or attitudes is much older than Descartes, but the systematic division of the Universe into material and immaterial substance which accounted for such observations as following from a universal cosmology and which could explain which objects would have volitions and why, does belong to Descartes.

3. Parallel processing computers are formally equivalent to sequential machines. All are instantiations of some Turing machine. Subject to a few exceptions, anything that can be done by a parallel processing computer could, in principle, be done in the same time by a much faster sequential processor. The exceptions to this generalisation arise from those problems which could in theory be solved by a suitably powerful parallel processing machine but which are so complicated that a sequential processor capable of performing the same calculation in the same time would need to break some fundemental law of phisics. That is to say that this imaginary sequential processing machine would need to split the quantum unit of time in order to operate, or would be so vast as to collapse into a black hole, or suffer from some similar limitation. I believe that such limitations do not affect the conclusions of my arguments.

4. See discussion of Putnam, Dennett, Pylyshyn, and Fodor, below.

8

2 A review of the work of Putnam, Dennett, Fodor, Pylyshyn and Pollock

One

In his paper *Computational Psychology and Interpretation Theory*,[1] Hillary Putnam commits himself[2] to saying that the mind thinks with the aid of representations. He continues:

> Suppose we try to say : the mind understands without using representations what it is for snow to be white, and it knows the representation 'snow is white' is true if and only if that state of affairs holds. Not only does this treat the mind as something that 'knows' things, instead of analysing knowing into more elementary and less intentional processes, but it violates the fundamental assumption of cognitive psychology, that understanding what states are, thinking about them, etc., cannot be done without representations. At bottom, we would be stuck with the myth of comparing representations directly with unconceptualised reality.[Putnam 1987, p.5. His emphasis.]

I do want to say that the mind knows and understands without using representations (at least in Putnam's sense of the word). It is therefore important to see just why Putnam believes in representations.

It seems to me that Putnam's belief in representations arises very naturally out of his theory of language which he has articulated gradually and lucidly in a series of papers beginning in the early 1960s. This theory attempts to explain meaning in language in terms of its correspondence with possible worlds.

In his paper *Do true assertions correspond to reality?*[3] Putnam gives an account of sentences in natural language in terms of possible worlds. Putnam claims that there exists a unique natural mapping of well-formed (i.e. meaningful,) sentences onto the set of possible worlds, and that the set of possible worlds which corresponds[4] to a true sentence always contains the real world and that the set corresponding to a false sentence never contains the real world.

If Putnam is to succeed with this strategy he must give some account of possible worlds which is extra-linguistic; otherwise he will merely go round in circles inside language. To achieve this he articulates the notion of possible worlds in terms of functions which specify physical parameters (such as mass and charge), at all points in space. [5]

Having done this Putnam is in a position to adumbrate a theory of language. This is spread through two papers. [6] By the time he has finished he has shown - at least by his own lights - that the identification of meaningful language is an effectively computable process and has grounded it in a theory of truth which is itself grounded in the way the world is, or might be.

Which sentences are meaningful can now (on Putnam's account), be explained entirely in terms of rules which may be followed in a mechanical fashion (by this I mean rules that are effectively computable).

Putnam regards natural language as a formalised language. This means one that has grammatical rules that are effectively computable. Consequently it comes as no surprise to find that he expresses sympathy for the idea that thinking involves the manipulation of symbols which have the structure of a formalised language. [7] Since he regards natural language as formalised, it must be effectively computable and thus, assuming Church's thesis, Turing-computable. In another paper, *The nature of mental states*[8], Putnam puts forward the idea that human beings are probabilistic automata. [9] By this he means an instantiation of a Turing machine in which the state transition tables are defined in terms of probabilities. In the light of this it is not surprising to find that he is sympathetic to descriptions of thinking which see it as similar to some modern computer programs. Putnam's belief in representations and his sympathy for the A.I. account of persons can thus be seen as natural consequences of a theory of language, truth, and meaning which he has been articulating in bits since the early 1960s.

Putnam expands this idea of a mental state a little in a later paper. [10] His idea is that at least some thinking involves constructing a model of the world. To do this the mind needs to represent. This, he writes,[11] involves two ideas. The first is that thinking involves the manipulation of symbols which have the structure of a formalised language. The second (which would appear to follow from the first), is:

that the human mind thinks (in part,) by constructing some kind of 'model' of its environment: a 'model of the world'. This model need not, of course, literally resemble the world. It is enough that there should be some kind of systematic relation between items in the representational system and items 'out there', so that what is going on 'out there' can be read off from its representational system by the mind.[Putnam 1987, p.2. His emphasis.]

If I understand the notion of a model in this context correctly, what it amounts to is a collection of symbols and mappings between them which are said to be in the mind and which stand in a 1-1 correspondence to objects and relations in the world as defined by our interests. Putnam does give an example of what he means. He writes:

If we have a predicate, say F, which represents the relation bigger than... and if we have individual 'constants' or proper names, say a and b, which represent the cities Paris and Vienna..., then we can represent the fact that Paris is bigger than Vienna by just including in our list of accepted sentences (our 'theory of the world') the sentence Fab.[Putnam 1987, pp.2-3. His emphasis.]

Putnam goes on:

the open sentence which we write in the formal notation as 'Fxy' is correlated to the relation which holds between any two things if and only if they are both cities and the first is larger - in population - than the second.[Putnam 1987, pp.2-3.]

Such a concept of representation and formal models would seem to be subject to powerful objections about how a person may, on this account of mind, be reasonably sure that he is not suffering from a systematic confusion between, say, what he perceives as a table and what he perceives as a chair. Putnam, it seems to me, does not give us enough detail to be able to follow up such a suspicion. He continues his account by suggesting that the connection between formal language and representations is much closer than what is required to render meaningfulness of sentences effectively computable (and thus describable by automata theory). He sees formalised language as being the medium of representation and of computation. He writes:

When our 'representational system' is itself a theory, and when our method of employing our representational system involves making formal deductions, we see that one and the same object - the formalised language including rules of deduction - can be the formalised language that computer scientists have been led to postulate as the brain or mind's (the difference does not appear particularly significant from this perspective) medium of computation, and, simultaneously, the medium of representation. The mind uses a formalised language

11

(or something like a formalised language) both as a medium of computation and as a medium of representation.[Putnam 1987, p.3. His emphasis.]

Two ideas stand behind this, both of which Putnam credits12 to computer scientists working in Artificial Intelligence and Cognitive Psychology. The first is that the process in the machine by which it arrives at a result (e.g. 'move this lever', or 'output that symbol',) must proceed by rules of inference applied to symbols which have the structure of a formalised language. (I.e. The meaningfulness of any given sentence of symbols is effectively computable - assuming Church's thesis.)

The second is that the machine has a collection of sentences of symbols in the formalised language which stand in a systematic (usually 1-1,) relation to the world. This he calls a 'model of the world'. 13 Putnam's idea, expressed in the quote, is that it is possible to define the symbols of the formalised language and the rules of inference for use upon it in such a way that this same thing is also a 'model of the world'. Thus he hypothesises that the mind uses a formalised language both as a medium of computation and as a medium of representation. It follows from Putnam's hypothesis that thinking is a process which goes forward by means of manipulating a formalised language according to rules of inference.

This tidies up a number of problems for Putnam very neatly. In some of his earliest published work[14] he demonstrates that it is probable that meaningfulness of language is effectively computable (and that natural languages are therefore probably formal languages). This is sufficient to demonstrate that it is probable that the mind has a medium of representation adequate for representing the world. The medium must be adequate for representing the world because natural language is adequate for representing the world, and it is the meaningfulness (or lack of it), that gets computed within the medium of computation.[15]

The role played by formalised language here makes thinking potentially independent of the human body; for formalised languages are an abstract mathematical idea, and any formalised language may have many, and quite distinct, instantiations. By adopting such a position Putnam commits himself to the idea that a suitably constructed and programmed box of electronics with suitable transducers could think.

Putnam does seem to want to say something like this. The thrust of his paper,[16] is to show that while he believes that the mind contains representations, nonetheless, these will need interpretation before they can be understood because what they represent will be relative to the interests of the person in question. He sees belief and desire as being interest relative and thus 'holistic'. By this he means that they can only be understood and ascribed in circumstances which take into account the whole person and their situation. Thus he writes:

> The point of my argument...is that there may be sentence analogues and predicate analogues in the brain, but not concepts.[Putnam 1987, p.17 His emphasis.]

In the light of what he has written earlier in this paper, about proper names which represent the cities of Paris and Vienna and the relation 'bigger than', the notion of interpretation in use here is unclear. Either there is a 1-1 correspondence between representations (in this sense) and objects in the world, or there is not. If there is, then for discourse about objects and their relation to one another Putnam is committed to a version of the mentalese hypothesis. This is the hypothesis that the brain (and, in this hypothesis, the mind), operates by use of a formalised language analogue. Thus anything which can occur in normal language can have an analogue in the brain. This includes concepts. If there is no such 1-1 a correspondence then it is unclear what use is served by the talk about formalised languages, for the meanings of the proper names and their relations to each other will then be determined by the interpretation. The formal aspect of the language which is central to Putnam's thinking, which guarantees that meaningfulness is effectively computable, is now redundant. Putnam does not expand on this idea of interpretation. Consequently the paper17 renders this aspect of his public position obscure.

From this brief survey we can see that Putnam's belief that representations are involved in thinking flowed quite naturally (but not inevitably), from a paper in the early 1960s in which he espoused the idea that the grammatical rules for any language are effectively computable. He then articulated a theory of meaning which attempted to ground meaning in structure and grammar. This led him to believe that the determination of meaningfulness of language is effectively computable. With this in mind it seems quite natural that he should look to the general theory of computability (Turing algorithms and automata theory), to explain how minds work when they are concerned with anything meaningful. This amounts to saying that mentation is closely analogous to some kind of computer program in operation. From this, and the observation that a formalised language with reference definitions can be both a medium of computation and simultaneously a medium of representation, it is a small step to say that minds use representations for much of thinking. After all, once one has accepted that minds are significantly similar to an operating computer program, that they need representations to be more than a formal aspect of behaviouristic automata, and that the medium of computation could also be a medium of representation, it would seem obtuse not to suppose that minds employ representations for much of their activity.

For later reference I would note here that Putnam is clearly committed to the idea that the computer metaphor and a certain concept of process drawn from the study of computers play a crucial part in giving answer to the question 'What is mind?'.

Two

D.C. Dennett is probably the best known exponent of the computational metaphor. His account is begun in *Content and Consciousness*[18] and continued in *Brainstorms: Philosophical essays on mind and psychology*[19] and *The Intentional Stance*[20]. He has also published various other papers which are not collected in these volumes.

The first chapter of *Content and Consciousness* is taken up with a discussion of ontology, mind, science, existence, identity, and grammar as they apply to philosophical problems about mind. The fundamental motivating thought which lies behind all this is closely connected to Putnam's original motivation, namely that if it were possible to give some quite general explanation, such as a grammar, by which we could determine which sentences are malformed and which are not, and which sentences are true and which ones are false, then many of the traditional problems of philosophy of mind would be solved or dissolved. (A malformed sentence is one which consists of meaningful words arranged in accordance with conventional grammar, but which is nonetheless meaningless. An example given by Dennett is that in talking about doing something 'for Smith's sake' it makes no sense to ask 'How old is Smith's sake?'.) Thus Dennett writes:

> Our task is... to pinpoint those conditions that can be relied upon to render the whole of the sentence 'Tom is thinking of Spain' true or false.[Dennett 1969, p.18]

This ambitious idea owes something to Gilbert Ryle and in particular his book The Concept of Mind. 21 Dennett hopes that by giving a quite general explanation of which sentences are malformed he will be able to say which categories and which ways of speaking are appropriate for words and phrases such as 'pain', 'hope', 'fear', 'for the sake of', and similar things. Dennett construes this22 as part of a broader programme to find how sentences containing such words and phrases can be correlated in an explanatory way with sentences drawn solely from the referential domain of the physical sciences.

Dennett notes23 that this programme need not commit him to find among the things of science any referents for the terms of mental vocabulary (this would only become necessary if some mental terms resisted all attempts to treat them as non-referential). It would be sufficient to find those conditions, expressed in the language of science, which reliably render the whole of a sentence such as 'Tom is thinking of Spain.' true or false.

Dennett then proceeds to consider the problems presented by modern accounts of intentionality for this stance. The challenge of intentionality amounts to an argument that certain sentences concerned with mental attitudes or states are true or false in virtue of certain features of the world which are outside of the domain of the physical sciences and cannot be expressed in the language of science. Clearly if such an argument were correct there could not be the kind of explanatory mapping of sentences containing mental vocabulary onto sentences from the language of the physical sciences for which Dennett hopes.

Dennett gives an account[24] of the intentional as a mark of the mental. In doing so he follows Chisholm's reworking of Bretano. He is concerned to note that intentionality of a sentence amounts to saying that the sentence is intensional. By intensional (with an 's'), he means non-extensional, that is, not following the rules of extensional, truth functional, logic. He considers various arguments for the claim that there are intensional sentences (i.e. ones whose sense can never be replaced by an extensional sentence or paraphrase). The one that he finds most powerful he ascribes to Quine[25]. This arises out of a consideration of cases of indirect quotation (i.e. 'X says that P'). For example, 'X says that it is raining'. If the sense of this sentence can be reproduced by an extensional sentence or paraphrase, then there must be some class of physical states of affairs which would be in force always and only when someone was saying that it was raining. Reflection suggests that there cannot be such a class; and if there is no such class for so overt a matter as saying that it is raining, how can we think that there might be such a class for more hidden and private phenomena such as believings and imaginings. Dennett also notes however,[26] that since this is a negative existential claim it can never be absolutely established, but only made extremely compelling.

All this makes very plausible, but does not prove, the intentionalists' claim that no sentence can be found which adequately reproduces the information of an intentional sentence and still conforms to extensional logic. This would appear to doom Dennett's programme. He writes:

> The effect of the intentionality thesis is to give the old, ill-envisaged, dogma that the mind cannot be caged in a physical theory a particularly sharp set of teeth.[Dennett 1969, p.39]

Dennett's answer arises from his observation[27] that the argument for irreducibility depends on the lack of theoretically reliable overt clues for the ascription of intentional expression. This, he says, leaves room for covert internal events serving as the condition for ascription. Such data could not serve as our ordinary criteria for the use of intentional expression because we do not ordinarily have access to such data. This however does not undermine the possibility in principle of producing a scientific reduction of intentional expression to extensional expression about internal states.

Dennett suggests[28] that people might have a system of internal states or events the extensional description of which could be upgraded to an intentional system. This is a position in tension with that which he takes in *Brainstorms*. There[29] he explains that there would be no need for a reduction of mentalistic talk if we could legitimise such talk by providing it with rules of attribution and exhibiting its predictive power. Dennett's project has undergone a considerable change between these two books. In *Content and Consciousness*[30] the programme was to find an explanatory correlation between mentalistic sentences and those drawn solely from the referential domain of the physical sciences. In *Brainstorms*[31] it is to provide rules of attribution for, and to exhibit the predictive power of, mentalistic talk. Insofar as an explanatory correlation would provide rules of attribution the earlier project might be conceived of as a special case of the later project

Despite these changes in definition the basic hope that he sets out in *Content and Concsiousness*[32] that covert internal events might serve as the condition for ascription of intentional expression remains. The crucial question must now be 'What justifies such ascriptions?'

Dennett sets about answering this in *Content and Consciousness* by reference to evolution. He notes[33] that a computer can only be said to be believing, remembering, perceiving, and so on relative to the particular interpretation put upon its motion by people. In doing so they impose the intentionality of their own way of life on the computer. That is to say that Dennett thinks that if a machine can be said truly to be inspecting a light bulb, it can only be said to be doing so in virtue of having been designed to do precisely this or things of which inspecting a light bulb is an instance. Otherwise it would not be inspecting a light bulb but malfunctioning in some way. Insofar as computers are intentional they are intentional in virtue of the intentionality of their creators. People and animals however are not designed and manufactured in the way that computers and their programs are, nor are they essentially in the service of interpreting, intentional beings. Thus there would seem to be a fundamental difference between human and animal intentionality and that which we might ascribe to a computer.

Dennett suggests that we should think of ourselves and animals as having been endowed with intentionality by natural selection. He observes[34] that over the long run natural selection guarantees the environmental appropriateness of antecedent-consequence connections in people. Intentional description presupposes this appropriateness of antecedent-consequence connections. Thus natural selection guarantees what intentional description presuppose. If environmental appropriateness is sufficient for appropriate intentional description, then natural selection guarantees this also. Thus for Dennett what justifies intentional descriptions is the environmental appropriateness of these descriptions. For example, 'John is afraid', would be a justified description of John if John's behaviour was that of being afraid in a context or environment in which we could make sense of his being afraid.

In taking this view Dennett is implicitly contradicting those like Chisholm (Dennett names such people The Intentionalists') who believe that intentional phenomena are absolutely irreducible to physical phenomena and that intentional sentences cannot be reduced to or paraphrased into extensional sentences about the physical world. Therefore, for that account, no sentence or sentences can be found which adequately reproduce the information of an intentional sentence and still conform to extensional logic.

Against the Intentionalists' claim (which as I noted above, page 15, can never be fully demonstrated), and in the light of his earlier discussion[35] of the ontological problems of mind, Dennett can reply that his kind of account has a minimum of assumptions, in particular a minimal ontology, is consistent with our knowledge of the world, particularly our scientific knowledge, and, if it could be successfully fleshed out, would have considerable explanatory power.

Such a position makes it tempting to think of persons as closely analogous to computers. Dennett does indeed do just this. He writes of

the remarkable and fruitful analogy between the logical states of a

Turing machine and the mental states of a human being, on the one hand, and the structural states of a Turing machine and the physical states of a human being, on the other.[Dennett 1969, p.102]

He pursues this analogy with an account of how a machine might be made introspectively incorrigible. This leads him to say[36] that a sentence uttered is not a description of a cerebral event but the expression of the event's content. As a description it is subject to verbal errors, but not to misdescription or misidentification. Thus he writes that the intentional characterisation of an event or state (which identifies it as the event or state with a certain content), fixes its identity in almost the same was as a machine table description fixes the identity of a logical state. The intentional characterisation, however, only alludes to the further states whereas the machine table characterisation determines it completely.[37]

The position that Dennett argues for, at least in *Content and Consciousness*, is that the condition for the correct ascription of intentional predicates, phrases, and sentences to a person is that the person should have appropriate internal states. The criterion for such ascriptions is that in the environmental context, such ascription is appropriate. The crucial part of this, the relationship between internal states and environmentally justified internal ascriptions, is to be sorted out by means of the programme on which Dennett has embarked.

This does not lead Dennett to attempt to identify intentionally characterised brain processes with particular mental events or states. The reason he gives is that thoughts are 'What is reported' (i.e. the reported thing,) and therefore cannot be identified with what is reported (the subject of the report, i.e. what the reported thoughts are about), and since machine states are sub-personal they cannot be 'What is reported' (because thoughts, which in this case are the reported thing, are at a personal level).

Dennett does however identify some thought with information processing: He notes[38] that diligent and purposeful reasoning takes time, can leave us exhausted, go astray, be difficult, and bog down, and can thus be described as a process. He also believes that information processing must have gone on in thinking because information which is stored in a person has contributed to the organisation of the mind that reached the conclusion.[39] He knows it has contributed to the conclusion because without it he could not have reached the conclusion. Thus on Dennett's account purposeful and diligent reasoning is correctly described as information processing.

In his next book, *Brainstorms*,[40] Dennett describes himself[41] as a 'homuncular functionalist'. By this he means that he is quite happy with theories that posit 'little men' inside the mind to explain the properties of mind because he believes that they in turn can be analysed in terms of simpler homunculi which can then be analysed and that this can be repeated until in the end one is left with mechanical processes. Dennett writes:

> Eventually this nesting of boxes within boxes lands you with homunculi so stupid (all they have to do is remember to say yes or no when asked) that they can be, as one says, "replaced by a machine". One *discharges* fancy homunculi from ones scheme by organising armies of such idiots to do the work.[Dennett 1979, p.124 His emphasis.]

This is part of the answer Dennett espouses to a problem he names 'Humes Problem'. [42] I want to examine this in more detail because it makes clear that the explanatory role that Dennett sees for homunculi and representations is different to that which Putnam sees for his representations.

Dennett describes 'Humes Problem' in two parts: The first is a premise:

> The only psychology that could be possibly succeed in explaining the complexities of human activity must posit internal representations.[Dennett 1979, p.119]

This premise is justified by saying that it has seemed obvious to just about everyone except the radical behaviourists (amongst whom he lists Ryle and Malcolm). He cites as examples of internal representations from various theories 'ideas', 'sensations', and 'impressions' (from the British Empiricists), and 'hypotheses', 'maps', 'schemas', 'images', 'propositions', and 'engrams' (from cognitive psychology and various functionalist theories).

The second part of 'Humes problem' is the observation that:

> Nothing is intrinsically a representation of anything; something is a representation only *for* or *to* someone; any representation or system of representations thus requires at least one *user* or *interpreter* of the representation who is external to it.[Dennett 1979, p.122]

In order to use the representation any such interpreter must comprehend, and have beliefs and goals. Thus the interpreter is a sort of homonculus. Dennett sums up 'Humes Problem' by writing:

> Therefore, psychology *without* homunculi is impossible. But psychology *with* homunculi is doomed to circularity or infinite regress, so psychology is impossible.[Dennett 1979, p.122]

Dennett is cautious about committing himself wholly to the 'stupid homonculus' solution to Humes Problem, however he does write:

I think A.I. has broken the back of an argument [He means Humes Problem.] that has bedevilled philosophers and psychologists for over two hundred years.[Dennett 1979, p.119]

Notwithstanding his caution, it is clear from the passages quoted above concerning Humes Problem that Dennett sees homunculi and representations together as candidates to explain what beliefs, knowledge, understanding, desire, hopes, and goals are. [43] At no point however, in *Brainstorms*, does Dennett give a clear account of what he thinks representations might be or be like. He does assert[44] that the premise that there are internal representations is quite invulnerable, and that it has an impressive mandate. (He does not spell this mandate out but refers the reader , via one of his reviews[45] of the book to *The Language of thought* by J.A. Fodor.[46] The arguments for representations in the book consist largely of attacks, - some of them ill-considered, as Dennett points out in his review, - on any account which denies that there are internal representations.)

In taking this position Dennett is much bolder than Putnam. In Putnam representations are only required to explain beliefs, knowledge, and understanding. Putnam is much less sure about desires, hopes, and goals. Dennett, however, despite his caveats, sees the combination of representations with homunculi as explaining what all these things are. [47,48]

By the time Dennett comes to write on representations in 1987, in *The Intentional Stance*,[49] his enthusiasm for the computer metaphor seems to have waned a little. He gives quite a sympathetic account of G. Ryle's theories. In this paper he draws a useful distinction between what he calls explicit representations, implicit representations, and tacit representations. He defines explicit representations:

Information is represented *explicitly* in a system if and only if there actually exists in the functionally relevant place in the system a physically structured object, *a formula* or *string* or *tokening* of some members of a system (or "language") of elements for which there is a semantics or interpretation, and a provision (a mechanism of some sort,) for reading or parsing the formula.[Dennett 1987, p.216]

He defines implicit representation:

for information to be represented *implicitly* we shall mean that it is *implied* logically by something that is stored explicitly.[Dennett 1987, p.216]

20

Dennett then points out that with this definition, 'implicit' does not mean potentially explicit because all the logical implications of what is stored explicitly cannot be derived in finite time.

Dennett does not give so clear a definition of 'tacit representation'. Indeed the only basis I can see for calling such things representations at all is that it gives rise to an elegant triplet of forms of representation. He says that what he means by 'tacit' is what G. Ryle meant when he claimed that explicitly proving things (for example on a blackboard) depends on an agent having a lot of knowledge which could not be explained in terms of explicit representations because that would lead to infinite regress. (I suspect that this notion of tacit knowledge is either the same as or similar to Wittgenstein's notion of a technique.) Dennett is concerned in this paper to point out that "explicit depends on tacit". [50] He takes as an example a pocket calculator. He points out that it can deliver explicit representations of an infinite number of mathematical truths which are not stored within it. To do this the calculator does not look up a set of stored rules and then deduce the answers, rather it operates as it was designed to do as a consequence of its structure. Thus the arithmetical truths that it exhibits are not stored implicitly in it, rather they are stored tacitly in its structure and are potentially explicit.

Dennett goes on to point out[51] that such systems of tacit representations do not need to have terms which are in some sense translated into explicit representations, rather, tacit representation is simply tacit.

What Dennett is getting at here is that there is no need for the information which is represented tacitly to be other than an apparently mechanical mode of reaction. He gives the examples[52] of 'Now I am in my grandmothers house', and 'Now there is a distinct danger of being attacked by a predator approaching from the north-northeast'. His point is that one and the same system (the same bits of mechanism if you like), in different states can react quite differently and there is no requirement that predators or grandmothers or anything else at all will have been explicitly represented within the machine. Quite simply, when the machine is in such and such a state we would say that it thinks it is in its grandmother's house. What makes the state one of thinking it is in its grandmother's house (or of believing itself to be in danger of being attacked), is the role that the state plays for the machine. Thus Dennett writes:

States of such a system get their semantic properties directly and only from their globally defined functional roles.[Dennett 1987, p.223][53]

By introducing the notion of tacit representation Dennett has moved a long way from the position he held in *Brainstorms* when discussing Humes Problem.[54] There internal representations were said to be an 'invulnerable premise' and to have an 'impressive mandate'. Tacit representations are not, in any sense, a form of internal representation, rather they are some consequence of the physical structure of the machine. By introducing this idea Dennett has weakened, perhaps fatally, the computer metaphor in his scheme; for the explanatory correlation between intentional description and sentences expressible in the language of the physical sciences which he set out to find in Content and Consciousness, was to go forward by reference to internal events and states as conditions for the ascription of intentional predicates. It was as the only well worked out theory of such states that the computer metaphor was introduced. Now, it seems, he wants to say that the 'representations' to which homunculi or internal processes may make reference or which may figure in the explanatory correlation include the structure of the machine. It would seem then, that part of what makes it true that 'John is afraid' is that he has the right kind of structure for us to be able, correctly, to apply these words. Having the right kind of structure is not, in the sense Dennett used the words earlier, a 'covert' internal state.[55] If I have misunderstood Dennett and he does indeed mean something covert by tacit representations then he does not say why he wants to confine this idea to hidden structures. In Content and Consciousness the theory of evolution is invoked as a guarantor that animals and persons will be capable of having appropriate internal states for the ascription of intentional sentences. This appropriateness is, amongst other things, a matter of internal structure. Evolution affects all aspects of the structure of the typical bodies of animal species, both the overt and the covert aspects. Tacit representations will be representations which, at least in part, animals have in virtue of their evolutionary history. At no point does Dennett suggest that this notion of tacit representations is to be confined to covert bodily structures or to structural characteristics which are not determined by chemical genetics (such as neural interconnections in the brain). Indeed it would seem arbitrary if he did so limit this notion. Thus it seems that we must understand tacit representations as an evolved, physical, structural characteristic of any organism which has them. This seems to leave the computer metaphor behind.

It is now clear that some of the representations to which Dennett's homunculi will have access consist in bodily structures. Since representations on Dennett's account play a crucial role in explaining what an intentional state is, correct ascription of intentional sentences may now require that the thing to which they are ascribed should have an appropriate overt structure. This is only a short step from saying that intentional descriptions can only be applied to things with the appropriate form. This profound change of position by Dennett would seem to close off any avenue towards building an artificial person which he seemed at one time to be in the process of mapping. What he might possibly say is that if something with appropriate covert and overt structures were built then these would cause it to behave in a manner which would lead us to call it a person.

Despite his extensive writings on mind, artificial intelligence, and cognitive psychology Dennett avoids explicit commitment to any one theory or view. He does not write that he believes the mind to contain representations but that he cannot see any other possible source of explanation for mind. He is similarly committed on most other related subjects. He remains at least as much a commentator on other people's work as an originator of ideas about or approaches to mind.

In summary then, Dennett's position arises from an attempt to give an account of what mind is which takes full account of the observations and arguments of modern intentionalists and which is still fully compatible with ontological monism. This leads him to suggest that there are internal states in the brain or body the extensional description of which could be upgraded to an intentional discription.[56] Dennett is happy with the idea that anything that has a sufficiently rich repertoire of internal states could in principle be the subject of intentional ascriptions with just as much accuracy as humans are. Dennett notes that the theory of Turing Machines is the only well worked out theory of the internal states of machines. He also notes many instructive (to his way of thinking), parallels between programs which run on computers (which are themselves instantiations of the abstract concept of a universal Turing machine), and aspects of mind. In consequence of this, and because he finds no other theory plausible, Dennett (in both *Content and Consciousness* and in *Brainstorms*), comes to write about and think of mind more and more in terms of the computer metaphor. In these two books Dennett deduces that reasoning must, at least sometimes, be a form of information processing. He says it is a process because it has properties like a process, (e.g. it can take a long time, go astray, leave us exhausted, and so on,) and he reasons that the mind must store and process information because it can exhibit conclusions which would require that information for their rational deduction.

The later Dennett, particularly in his paper *Styles of Representation*,[57] hedges his position in such a way that his commitment to the computer metaphor must now come into question. For the attraction of the computer metaphor was that one metaphor might provide us with a completely general explanation of mind and of our 'mentalistic' language by means of correlating 'mentalistic' language with the language of the paradigm sciences. If the computer metaphor is now to be demoted to the status of an idea that is appealed to when needed to help explain particular aspects of mind then its attraction is greatly diminished, for computers do not have the least physical resemblance to anything that we know to have a mind.

The position I shall argue for is one that Dennett would find uncongenial. My case will be first that explicit and implicit representations are unnecessary to account for inner life. Second, that something similar to what he calls tacit representations (which are not representations in the normal sense of the word), are, when understood in a social contest, sufficient to explain what our inner lives are and to answer many of our questions about mind, and third that anything that is a person must have an appropriate history.

Three

Zennon W. Pylyshyn writes from the perspective of computer science rather than philosophy. He is the most philosophically minded and well informed of such writers that I have come across. He sets out his commitment to and grounds for believing in representations in a paper entitled *Computation theory and Cognition: Issues in the foundations of cognitive science*.[58]

Pylyshyn is a computational functionalist and claims that:

> The hierarchical character of programs and the abstraction represented by the information processing level of analysis make it the ideal vehicle for expressing functional models of all kinds.[Pylyshyn 1980, p.113]

The starting point (but not the motivation), for Pylyshyn's account is much the same as Dennett's, namely those minor philosophical problems that become urgent philosophical issues when one abandons dualism. Pylyshyn expresses this[59] by saying that there is a puzzle which arises because, while we believe that people do things because of their goals

24

and beliefs, we nonetheless also believe that this process is carried out by a causal sequence of events that can respond only to the intrinsic physical properties of the brain.

Pylyshyn notes[60] that the manner in which brain processes (which he believes to be involved in cognition), can depend on both the properties of brain tissue and on some other quite different domain such as chess or mathematics could be similar to the manner in which the state transitions of a computer can depend both on physical laws and on the abstract properties of numbers. This he says happens because both numbers and rules relating to numbers are represented in the machine as symbolic expressions and programs, and that it is the physical realization of these representations that determines the machine's behaviour. The abstract numbers and rules are first expressed in terms of syntactic operations over symbolic expressions or some notation for the number system and these expressions are then 'interpreted' by the built-in functional properties of the physical device. The machine does not interpret the symbols as numbers but only as formal patterns that cause the machine to function in some particular way.

This analogy between the brain and hardware and between mentation and software has been widely used, however Pylyshyn's exposition of it is exceptionally clear. It also begs many questions. Pylyshyn answers a few of these along the way.

Pylyshyn writes[61] that the fundamental reason why cognition ought to be viewed as computation is that computation is the only worked out view of process that is both compatible with a materialist view of how a process is realised and that attributes the behaviour of the process to the operation of rules upon representations. Thus, for Pylyshyn, the grounds for viewing both computation and cognition as processes of fundamentally the same type lies in their similarities: Both are physically realised, both are governed by rules and representations, both exhibit the same sort of dual character with respect to providing explanations of how they work, (i.e. the working of computers tends to be explained in terms of software and hardware, and the working of mind tends to be explained in terms of mental language and in terms of the functioning of the brain,) both can be understood as exhibiting this dual character for the same reasons and, to top it all, we have only one worked out theory of this kind of process and that is the theory of computation.

This list can seem impressive, but so would a list of the differences between computation and cognition. The important claim by which this account must be judged is that it can give a satisfactory explanation of the apparently dual nature of mental functioning. In this Pylyshyn is again close to Dennett .

Pylyshyn's explanation is that as a physical device the operation of a computer can be described in terms of the causal structure of its physical properties. In such a description the states of the computer are individuated in terms of the differences of their physical descriptions. The transitions between these states is therefore governed by physical laws. A functional description can also be given: In a functional description states are individuated by the systematic relations that hold over certain classes of physical properties. Typically these are very complex classes, such as the ones that correspond to the computationally relevant states of the computer. For example, one functional class might be that of 'adding 5 to 5'. This class will contain all those physical properties of the device which could pertain when the machine is adding 5 to 5. The membership criterion for this class will be something like those and only those physical properties which pertain when the device is 'adding 5 to 5'. This is a definition of a class of physical properties in terms of the function of its members. The transitions between such functionally defined states are no longer instances of a physical law, they are however reducible to some complex function of various physical laws and of the physical properties of the computer in its various states.

Pylyshyn's strategy is to attempt to provide two kinds of description of a computer which, with some refinement, will stand in relation to each other and to the computer as mentalistic talk and neurophysiological descriptions of the brain stand to each other and to the human body. The physical description of the states of the computer is to be understood as analogous to the neurophysical description of the brain, and the functional description as analogous to mentalistic talk about the mind. If Pylyshyn can make this strategy work, and in particular if he can make the functional description sufficiently similar to 'mentalistic' descriptions of people (describing their hopes, fears, thoughts, desires, reasons, etc.), then he will have given a very considerable boost to the computer metaphor, for he will have shown that in one case the same physical object can be described in two different ways which resemble the physical and mentalistic descriptions of persons.

Pylyshyn observes[62] that a computational process has no access to the actual represented domain itself. By this he means that a computer has no way of distinguishing whether a symbol represents a number, or a letter, or someone's name, or anything else. In this he admits a frequent criticism of the computer metaphor, namely that computational states do not represent at all (or as it is sometimes expressed a machine

26

'doesn't know what it is doing'). Pylyshyn writes,[63] that because a computational process has no access to the represented domain it is mandatory that all relevant semantic distinctions be mirrored by syntactic distinctions. In consequence semantic distinctions have to be mirrored by features which are intrinsic to the representation itself. [64]

What Pylyshyn is getting at here is that for two representations (or two anythings), to be distinguishable to the computer they must affect differently the way the computing process goes forward. This and only this can mark a distinction for such a process. Such a difference is what he means by a syntactic difference. In consequence, the only semantic difference that the machine will recognise will be those that are syntactically encoded. This leads Pylyshyn to write[65] that what we mean when we say that a device represents something is that the features of the representation will be reflected in functional differences in the operation of the device.

Pylyshyn notes[66] that it appears that certain regularities in behaviour can only be described in intentional terms. For example, when we talk about knowing how to get out of a building, or speak of people believing that a building is on fire, or speak of them having a goal of being out of the building, we attribute intentions to them which do not appear to be identifiably, even in principle, with particular causal sequences. A person will use their knowledge to determine a series of actions to satisfy such a goal. In general, when a person perceives himself to be in danger he will set about removing himself from the source of the danger. Such generalisations have an unlimited variety of instances, and each instance under a physical description could have an entirely different causal chain.

Such observations make it overwhelmingly likely that a conceptual analysis of cognitive phenomena will have to appeal to beliefs, goals, and all of intentional language. This would seem to show that representations of such things (which here are understood as machine representations and thus extensional), are not possible on this account.

To me it seems that Pylyshyn fails to resolve this objection adequately; despite having raised it himself. He does however give some clear pointers as to where he thinks the solution may be found.

Pylyshyn writes[67] that by separating the semantic and syntactic aspects of cognition we reduce the problem of accounting for meaningful action to the problem of specifying a mechanism that operates upon meaningless symbols or tokens, and in doing so carries out the meaningful process being modelled. He considers this a breakthrough because it makes it possible to view semantically interpreted rules as compatible with natural law.

The working machine can now be seen to be governed by natural law because the functional description is defined in terms of classes of physical properties, yet we can also see that the same machine states might have a different function on each occasion that it occurs. That is to say that the same machine states may correctly and consistently be interpreted as representing something quite different on each occasion of its occurrence. Thus the working of the machine (in the sense of what it is doing under a mechanical description), is completely independent of how its states are interpreted. For this reason Pylyshyn writes[68] that we can never specify the working of a computer unequivocally in terms of a semantically interpreted rule (such as 'this physical state represents the number five and the next will represent the number six').

On Pylyshyn's account so far computers would seem to be a poor candidate for a conceptual model from which we might hope to move forward and build a person because it seems that they can never 'know what they are doing'. By this I mean that, on Pylyshyn's account, computers are no more than vastly complex symbol manipulators in which the symbols have no intrinsic meaning. Meaning only arises from the functional role that we give to the operation of the machine. Pylyshyn does not attempt to do the work that Putnam and Dennett set out to do, of showing how we could justifiably ascribe meanings and intentions to a machine in the same way as we do to persons. Pylyshyn does however write[69] that it is far from clear whether a machine's working would remain completely independent of how its states were interpreted if it were wired up through transducers to a natural environment. The text does not make clear whether Pylyshyn thinks that in such a case some machine states might be shown to have particular specifiable meanings under such conditions or whether he thinks that in being wired up to transducers the states of the machine became meaningful and the machine thus comes to 'know what it is doing'.

This seems to me to be a crucial problem if any machine is to be a candidate for personhood, however Pylyshyn, like most other cognitive scientists seems to take the view that with enough empirical research such questions can be answered satisfactorily.

Pylyshyn does go on to say[70] that since the syntactic representation-governed nature of computation lends itself to describing cognitive processes in a way that makes their relation to causal laws bridgeable in principle, and since computation and cognition can be viewed in common abstract terms there is no reason why computation ought to be treated merely as a metaphor for cognition, rather it can be treated as an hypothesis about the literal nature of cognition. Indeed he goes on to write:

> If we view computation more abstractly as a symbolic process that transforms formal expressions that are in turn interpreted in terms of the domain of representation (such as numbers,) we see that the view that mental processes are computational can be just as literal as the view that what IBM computers do is properly viewed as computation.[Pylyshyn 1980, p.115]

Thus Pylyshyn ties himself very tightly indeed to the computational view of mind and of what it is that makes something a person.

In summary, Pylyshyn believes that cognition is computation because cognition and computation seem to him to have striking similarities and because he believes that such a view can solve the problems of dualism of explanation of behaviour. He succeeds in showing that a functional description of a device can be consistent with a description in terms of physical properties and physical laws without the functional description being itself law-governed. He does not begin to attack the much more difficult question of whether we may use intentional language of such devices in the same sense as we use it of persons.

It is clear from what I have quoted of Pylyshyn that he is totally committed to saying that the computer metaphor and talk of representations and process can answer the conceptual question 'What is mind?'.

My case against Pylyshyn will be that reflection upon the nature of representations must lead us to conclude that representations of the kind he is interested in cannot explain the puzzles they were invented to explain, and that much of cognition cannot sensibly be construed as any kind of process at all.

Four

In 1976 J.A. Fodor published a book entitled *The Language of Thought*.[71] In this he states clearly and argues for his views on the foundations of cognitive psychology. This book forms the basis for his later writing. Fodor believes that there is quite literally a language of thought (the kind of thing Dennett calls 'mentalese'), and that thinking is to be understood as a computational process in 'mentalese'.

Fodor opens chapter 1 of *The Language of Thought* with the words:

I propose, in this book, to discuss some aspects of the theory of mental processes.[Fodor 1976, p.1]

His commitment to processes in the mind could not be more clear. He immediately sets out to defend psychological theorising against what he calls reductionism. He writes:

The integrity of psychological theorising has always been jeopardised by two kinds of reductionism, each of which would vitiate the psychologists claim to study mental phenomena. For those influenced by the tradition of logical behaviourism, such phenomena are allowed no ontological status distinct from the behavioural events that psychological theories explain. Psychology is thus deprived of its theoretical terms except where these can be construed as nonce locutions for which behavioural reductions will eventually be provided. To all intents and purposes, this means that psychologists can provide methodologically reputable accounts only of such aspects of behaviour as are the effects of environmental variables.[Fodor 1976, p.1]

(The second kind of reductionism he refers to is 'physiological reductionism'. This will not concern me.)

This makes his motives clear, he feels that what he calls logical behaviourism threatens the status of psychology as an independent area of study.

Fodor goes on[72] to describe Wittgenstein and Ryle as logical behaviourists. He continues[73] that he has not space to mount a critique of Wittgenstein and procedes to launch into a critique of Ryle.

Fodor explains[74] that on Ryle's account what makes clowning clever is that it is done in public; that the clown does things that his audience does not expect, that the man the clown hit with a custard pie was wearing evening dress, and so on. Fodor notes that 1) none of these facts are in any way private, they are public, and 2) that on Ryle's account it is not the character of the *causes* of the clown's behaviour that make it clever clowning, but rather the character of the behaviour itself. Thus he writes that Ryle's central point is that 'cartesian' (which here means mentalistic) psychological theories treat what is really a logical relationship between aspects of a single event as though they were causal relations between distinct events. He writes:

It is this tendency to give mechanistic answers to conceptual questions which, according to Ryle, leads the mentalist to the orgies of regrettable hypostasis: i.e. to attempting to explain behaviour by reference to underlying psychological mechanisms.

If this is a mistake then I am in trouble. For it will be the pervasive assumption of my discussion that such explanations, however often they may prove to be empirically unsound are, in principle, methodologically impecable.[Fodor 1976, pp.6-7]

Fodor then sets out to refute Ryle's arguments. He gives an example to illustrate his point. He asks[75] 'What makes Wheaties the breakfast of champions?' (Wheaties being a breakfast cereal). Fodor asks us to suppose that Wheaties are indeed the breakfast of champions. Then, he says, there must exist a causal explanation for this. If there were not, Wheaties would be miraculous. There will also exist a conceptual explanation, such as that Wheaties is eaten by a non-negligible number of champions.

Fodor asks us to note[76] that the answers given by the conceptual story do not typically turn up in the causal story and vice versa. He stresses that the causal story and the conceptual story can be simultaneously true and that remarks about the conceptual story cannot replace the causal story. Indeed he writes:

...even if the behaviourists were right in supposing that logically necessary and sufficient conditions for behaviour being of a certain kind can be given (just) in terms of stimulus and response variables, that fact would not in the least prejudice the mentalistic claim that the *causation* of behaviour is determined by, and explicable in terms of, the organism's internal states.[Fodor 1976, p.8]

Fodor's concern is to show that there is a place for psychological theorising in 'mentalistic' terms which have such a status as not to be eliminatively reducible to behaviour. He writes:

I shall therefore assume, in what follows, that psychologists are typically in the business of supplying theories about the events that causally mediate the production of behaviour and that cognitive psychologists are typically in the business of supplying theories about the events that causally mediate the production of intelligent behaviour.[Fodor 1976, p.8]

Fodor seems to me to have got himself well and truly confused. To describe Ryle and Wittgenstein as logical behaviourists seems to me to be one confusion. To go on to ascribe theories about stimulus and response variables to Ryle is a further confusion, but his deepest confusion in this opening section of the book is to suppose that when a dietician explains that Wheaties is the breakfast of champions because it contains vitamins, that he is giving an explanation of exactly the

31

same thing as a philosopher who explains that Wheaties is the breakfast of champions because it is eaten by a non-negligible number of champions. If the dietician was giving an explanation of exactly the same thing as the philosopher then his explanation would simply be false. A person is a champion in virtue if winning competitions not in virtue of eating vitamins. Fodor is mistaken in thinking that the two explanations are in competition.

What the dietician's explanation is an explanation of is how to go about becoming a champion given that you live in a society with suitable institutionalised competitions, that you have certain skills, the appropriate motivation and so on. Under those circumstances a policy of eating Wheaties (according to the dietician), will help make you a champion. The dietician's explanation that what makes Wheaties the breakfast of champions is that it contains vitamins, cannot be a causal explanation of what it is to be a champion, despite being dressed up by the advertising agents to look like one. This example thus fails to illustrate the point it was intended to illustrate, namely "that both causal and conceptual stories can be simultaneously true, distinct answers to questions of the form: What makes (an) X (an) F"[77]

In Ryle's example of clever clowning there will, of course, be a causal explanation of the clown's movements. For this explanation the movements (of hand, arm, eye, mouth etc.) would be described in terms which are appropriate for, or capable of reduction to other terms appropriate for, a causal explanation. (E.g. Mass, momentum, velocity, etc.) These terms in which the causal explanation of what brought about the clown's movements is given, are quite different to the terms in which the conceptual explanation of what makes clowning clever is given (evening dress, custard pies, and so forth). There is thus no competition between these two explanations of the clever clowning. One is a conceptual answer to the conceptual question 'What made the clowning to be clever?', the other is a causal answer to a mechanical question, 'What caused the clown's movements?'. Further, a conceptual explanation of what makes the terms of the causal explanation (such as mass of the clown's arm, elasticity of his skin, momentum of custard pies etc.) to be the things that they are, will not need to make reference to the same circumstances (evening dress, position of custard pies etc.) as the conceptual explanation of what made the clowning to be clever. Thus there are no grounds for saying that ultimately, if we follow the chain of explanations of explanations backwards that we will find a causal story. The conceptual explanations are not in competition with the causal explanations.

It therefore seems to me that Fodor's defence of 'mentalistic' theorising fails. He needs to mount this defence in order to provide foundations for his broader project of giving an account of mental attributes as caused by computer-like processing of rules and representations of the world taking place in the brain.

Fodor follows his discussion of Ryle with a discussion of physiological reductionism and the unity of science. This leads him to conclude that straight reduction from the special sciences (such as Psychology), to the hard sciences (such as physics), is too strong a requirement in the face of the available evidence. He thinks however that there might be laws underlying generalisations in the special sciences which do not reduce because the kind predicates of the special sciences cross-classify the natural kinds of the physical sciences. [78]

Fodor then sets about advancing his theory proper. He begins with an account of making choices. He thinks that it is self-evident that organisms often believe the behaviour they produce to be behaviour of a certain kind and that explanations of the way the organism behaves often advert to the beliefs it has about its own behaviour. This he says makes his account of how behaviour is decided upon seem overwhelmingly plausible. He then gives an account of how at least some behaviour 'is decided upon'. He writes:

> The agent finds himself in a certain situation (S). the agent believes that a certain set of behavioural options ($B_1, B_2, B_3, ..., B_n$) are available to him in S; i.e., given S, B_1 through B_n are the things the agent believes that he can do. The probable consequences of performing each of B_1 through B_n are predicted; i.e., the agent computes a set of hypotheticals of roughly the form if B_i is performed in S, then, with a certain probability, C_i. Which such hypotheticals are computed and which probabilities are assigned will, of course, depend on what the organism knows or believes about situations like S. (It will also depend on other variables which are, from the point of view of the present model, merely noisy: Time pressure, the amount of compensation space available to the organism etc.) A preference ordering is assigned to the consequences. The organism's choice of behaviour is determined as a function of the preferences and the probabilities assigned.[Fodor 1976, p.28]

This is a model of how organisms make choices about their future behaviour which is based on standard mathematical decision theory.

Fodor goes on to describe this as 'a very central pattern of psychological explanation'[79] and to point out that it presupposes some sort of representational system. He writes:

> to use this sort of model is, then, to presuppose that the agent has

33

access to a representational system of very considerable richness. For, according to the model, deciding is a computational process; the act the agent performs is a consequence of computations defined over representations of possible actions. No representations, no computation. No computation, no model.[Fodor 1976, p.31]

This then explains why Fodor believes that the mind contains representations. In fact he goes much further in his use of them than is shown by this quotation: In a footnote[80] he explains that what distinguishes what organisms do from what planets do in following rules is that a representation of the rules that organisms follow constitutes one of the causal determinants of their behaviour whereas for planets this is not so. This, I think, implies that he must be committed to explicit representation, for otherwise the distinction he wishes to mark with this example is not clear. Thus for Fodor explicit representations are a causal determinant of action.

In 1981 Fodor published a collection of papers entitled *Representations*.[81] It is not surprising to find that it defends, amongst other things, the thesis that there exist explicit representations in the mind. Fodor's defence of this idea runs through most of the book. Much of the defence that he does offer consists in citing experimental findings in psychology and asking rhetorically 'How else are these things to be explained?'. This is, of course, a quite different approach to mind from the conceptual claims of *The Language of Thought*, which I have just discussed. The defence becomes quite explicit in the paper entitled *Propositional attitudes*.[82] In this paper Fodor's motivation seems close to that of Putnam. He is concerned with language and the problems posed by ambiguous sentences. He believes that the human capacity to sort out the correct meanings of ambiguous sentences is the key to understanding our capacity to understand language. He writes:

The general characteristics of propositional attitudes appear to demand sentence-like entities to be their objects. And broadly empirical conditions appear to preclude identifying these entities with sentences of *natural* language - hence internal representations and private languages.[Fodor 1981, p.198. His emphasis]

He continues:

the best accounts of mental processes we have are quite unintelligible unless something like the internal representations story is true.[Fodor 1981, p.198]

He argues for this in the following way: Fodor asks us to consider the ambiguity of the sentence 'They are flying planes'. He says that the conventional explanation of this ambiguity points out that there are two ways of 'bracketing' the sentence. The first gives an answer to the question 'What are those guys doing?' and the second to the question 'What are those things?'.

Let us call this sentence ('They are flying planes') 'S'. Fodor is critical of the usual account of ambiguity of 'S' (that it has two bracketings). This he says means that there exists a function (let us call it 'G'), which maps the word 'sentence' onto precisely those bracketed word strings which constitute the sentences of English. According to this account both of the possible bracketings of S and no others lie in the range of G.

Fodor criticises this explanation for being enthymemic. He thinks that when the other premise of the syllogism is stated it can be seen that it explains nothing. He seems to think (but does not explicitly state), that when unpacked this explanation amounts to 'S is an English sentence', all English sentences lie in the range of 'G', therefore 'S lies in the range of G'. Fodor asks how the mere, so to speak platonic, existence of G could account for the facts about the ambiguities of English sentences. Why, he asks, are there not other functions (for example G'), which give to the sentences other bracketings. How is the mere existence (in whatever sense) of G supposed to explain the linguistic properties of S?

Fodor answers this question in this way:

So far as I can see, theres only one way such questions can conceivably be answered - viz. by holding that G-proper (not only exists but) specifies the very system of (internal (what else?)) representations that English speakers/hearers use to parse the sentences of their language. But, then, if we accept this, we are willy - nilly involved in talking of at least some mental processes (processes of understanding and producing sentences) as involving at least some relations to at least some internal represntations.[Fodor 1981, p.200]

Thus for Fodor the normal human capacity for disambiguation gives evidence that a system of internal representations which English speakers use to parse the sentences of their language. The evidence for the existence of this system consists in the observation that only one mapping out of many possible ones which can be imagined is exhibited by reality. The evidence for its being a system of representations consists in the observation that propositional attitudes require things like sentences to be their objects, however since other considerations preclude sentences of natural language, the objects of propositional attitudes must be things that can be meaningful, like sentences of natural language, but are not sentences of natural language. These he says are representations. [83] The evidence that these representations are internal consists in the observation that they don't seem to be anywhere else.

Another way of taking Fodor's criticism of the usual explanations about ambiguity would be to see them as showing the absurdity of that style of explanation, however, he goes on to say of the representations account:

> ...the account is well evidenced, not demonstrably incoherent, and again, it is the only one in the field. A working science is ipso facto in philosophical good repute.[Fodor 1981, p.200]

Fodor does think[84] that it is conceivable that propositional attitudes are not relations to internal representations. He writes:

> the theory that propositional attitudes are relations to internal representations is a piece of empirical psychology, not an analysis. For there might have been angels, or behaviourism might have been true, and then the internal representations story would be false. The moral is, I think, that we ought to give up asking for analyses; psychology is all the philosophy of mind we are likely to get.[Fodor 1981, p.202]

This is a surprising statement in view of the preceding 200 or so pages. It now appears that Fodor's position is this: If there are any answers to be had to the philosophical problems of mind, then they are to be found through empirical work by psychologists. Thus insofar as there are answers to questions such as 'What is mind?' they are the answers given by psychology in whatever form is prominent at the moment of asking. For Fodor this means cognitive psychology with computational metaphor.

For Fodor, then, such questions are either unanswerable or to be answered by the computational metaphor.

Fodor's central motivation for this allegiance to the computer metaphor seems to arise from a fear that mentalistic explanation implies dualistic explanation unless some kind of reduction of the mentalistic explanation can be offered. He seems to think this because mentalistic explanation is often intentional explanation and he believes that intentional explanation is explanation in non-physical terms. He seems to think that an unreduced non-physical explanation must be a dualistic explanation. His project is to provide a non-eliminative reduction of intentional and thus mentalistic explanation to physical terms by means of the computer metaphor.

Having thus, in effect, set himself the task of finding some kind of coherent non-eliminative reduction of intentional explanation to physical explanation the computer metaphor is a natural way to procede. It certainly appears at first sight to be a promising route.

The computer metaphor offers a paradigm of systematic relationship between abstract properties (such as numbers or symbols), process, and physical devices which can accommodate complexity and functional diversity of a richness we usually associate only with people. The computer metaphor has the further satisfying quality that it is grounded in rigorous mathematical logical theory.

As with the other authors I have considered it is clear that for Fodor too the computer metaphor and talk of process and of representations is intended to answer the question 'What is mind?'.

My case against Fodor will be that it is not necessary to flee into computational psychology in order to avoid dualism, that there is a way of understanding Ryle and Wittgenstein which is neither dualistic nor barren, that his idea of representations leaves what it is that makes something to be a representation quite unclear, and that the mind does not contain representations in anything like the sense that he requires.

One point worth noting here is that if the account of an' internal language' and of 'representations' given by Fodor (and implied by Pylyshyn), were true, things that have minds would have their beliefs, knowledge, thoughts, and so forth independently of the forms of their realisation. In particular this would be independent of their body-form. I believe that I can show that this must be false. (see chapters 4 and 5 below.)

From all that I have written and quoted it is clear that Putnam, Dennett, Pylyshyn, and Fodor are all in varying ways committed to the existence of representations in the mind and to the idea that the computer metaphor with some concept of representations and of process form a central part of any acceptable answer to the question 'What is mind?'.

Five

The previous four authors that I have discussed have all been concerned in their own way to provide an account of mind based on the computer metaphor. The next author I want to criticise is John Pollock and in particular his book *How to build a person: A prologomenon.* [85] Pollock is concerned to explain how an artificial person might be built. I take his work to be a paradigm of the strong A.I. thesis and his style of argument to be representative of the most common form of the strong A.I. thesis.

The preface to this book opens with the following words:

> This book is a prologomena to the enterprise of building a person. It is a defence of three theses: token physicalism, agent materialism, and strong A.I.[Pollock 1989, p.IX]

He goes on, on the same page, to define token physicalism as the thesis that mental events are physical events and presumably neurophysiological events. Agent materialism he defines as the thesis that persons are physical objects having a suitable structure, and strong A.I. as the thesis that one can construct a person (a thing that literally thinks, feels, and is conscious), by building a physical system endowed with appropriate 'artificial intelligence'. He summarises his views:

> The central claim of the book is that building a person reduces to the task of constructing a system that adequately models human rationality.[Pollock 1989, p.IX]

Chapter 1 of the book opens with the words:

> My general purpose in this book is to defend the conception of man as an intelligent machine. Specifically I will argue that mental states are physical states and persons are physical objects.[Pollock 1989, p.1]

This is followed by a fable which is intended to encourage the view that the attitudes, puzzles, and possibilities that we have with respect to machines as persons might be held with equal justification by an engineer who had built a human being. This fable is not a formal argument, it simply presents fabulous machines as persons built by engineers. In passing, Pollock remakes Putnam's point that machines of this kind could arrive at a mind/body problem for themselves by a process of reasoning closely analogous to ones which can be used to set up the mind/body problem for human beings.[86]

He goes on[87] to describe token physicalism as a scientific hypothesis for which he believes there is overwhelming evidence. He does not intend to present an a priori argument for token physicalism. The precise thesis he defends is "that all mental state tokens are also physical state tokens".[88] He gives as an example of a mental state token a particular instance of a specific person being in pain. He claims that such events as having a particular sensation, thought, or quale (rather than the particular sensation, thought, or quale themselves), are identical with some physical event.

Pollock seems to think that all he has to do in order to make token physicalism plausible is to show that what he calls "the felt quality of mental states",[89] such as the feeling of pain, could be present as a consequence of a purely physical state. To this end he distinguishes[90] between sensations and the feel of sensation. The feel of sensation he analyses as introspective sensation. By way of an example he asks how the sensation of feeling a rock could be the same as the feel of the sensation of feeling a rock. He writes:

> The feel of the rock is what we get when we inspect the rock, and it is most natural to regard the feel of the sensation as that we get when we inspect the sensation. That is precisely the view of sensation I am now advocating. To inspect the sensation is to employ your introspective sensors.[Pollock 1989, p.15]

This division of our senses into pairs is supposed to hold for all our senses.

He then suggests that the feel of a sensation being different from the sensation fits quite well into our normal mental life. He points out that in normal sense perception we are aware of our surroundings but are unaware of our sensations. When we are not attending to our sensations we are not aware of them. He goes on[91] to suggest an explanation of blindsight (a disorder in which a person may believe themselves blind or partially blind, yet be able to point, when asked, to objects in the blind part of their visual field), as a situation where the capacity for introspective sensing of vision has been lost but the capacity for vision itself has not.

Having argued in this fashion for conceptual separation of our traditional senses into pairs of senses he then argues that we should believe this account to be true. He sets about this by arguing that token physicalism is true. The structure of his argument is to show that token physicalism could be true because the separation of our senses into introspective and sensational senses removes the standard objections to token physicalism, and then to argue for the truth of token physicalism. This he does by what he calls The Causal Nexus Argument.

This goes as follows:

(1) Mental and physical events are involved in a single causal nexus. - There are causal paths leading from the mental to the physical, (e.g. I raise my arm,) and there are causal paths leading from the physical to the mental, - sensations etc. (Throughout this argument 'causal' is to be taken to mean lying in law-like relation to something.)

(2) Insofar as physical events have a causal ancestry, that ancestry can be described in purely physical terms.

(3) This requires an explanation and, he asserts, the most plausible explanation is that mental events are physical events. [92]

He also claims that if the logical structures of this Causal Nexus Argument is applied to visual and tactile sense then it gives us grounds to hold it reasonable to believe that our visual sense and our tactile sense give us information about the same world. Therefore, he seems to think, because the logical structure is the same, the Causal Nexus Argument in the form we have just examined gives us ground to hold it reasonable to believe that mental (by which he means introspective), sensing and physical sensing also give us information about the same world. He sees this parallel because he believes introspection to be a form of sensing of other senses. He writes:

> The only difference between the preceding reasoning [He means the Causal Nexus Argument.] and the reasoning underlying the visual/tactile identity thesis is that the data being explained consist of the premises of the Causal Nexus Argument rather than an observed mental/physical isomorphism. Presumably the latter is there to be found, but we havn't found it yet.[Pollock 1989, p.19]

He does not spell out the application of the Causal Nexus Argument to visual/tactile isomorphism, so I have tried to reconstruct it.

My reconstruction runs as follows:

(1) Visual and tactile events are involved in a single visual/tactile isomorphism. - Things that are tactilely round appear round (visually), and things that are visually round usually feel round (tactilely).

(2) Insofar as roundness has an explanation that explanation can be given in purely physical terms.

(3) This requires an explanation and the most plausible explanation is that visual perception and tactile perception both perceive the same physical worlds.

Thus Pollock thinks that because (so he says), this argument makes it reasonable to believe that our tactile and visual senses sense the same physical world an argument of the same structural form will make it reasonable to believe that mental events are physical events. He thinks this because he can describe mental events as a form of sensing of sensing.

This completes Pollock's defence of token physicalism. Even if we accept his account of the Causal Nexus Argument, the defence he offers might be precised as: Token physicalism is attractive. If we re-jig the way we think about mental events then we can get round the standard counter examples and objections. This is a good enough reason for believing the re-jigged account of 'token physicalism.'

Pollock next sets out to defend agent materialism[93]. This, he says, is the thesis that people are physical objects. [94] As with token physicalism he regards agent materialism as a well confirmed scientific hypothesis.

The structure of his argument is to define what he calls 'De Se Thought', then to argue that De Se beliefs are necessary for the computations he believes are involved in normal human activity, that a capacity for De Se thinking is sufficient to explain consciousness, and for correct re-identification of individual persons on the different occasions of meeting them. Pollock does not however, identify people with their bodies, rather he says they supervene on their bodies. This he says explains how it is that a person can die without the body going out of existence, and is what one would expect because almost all physical objects 'supervene on their substrates' or the substance of which they are made.

De Se thought, as explained by Pollock, is thought about something, possibly oneself, relative to oneself. The example he asks us to consider is of someone in a supermarket noticing that someone has a hole in a bag of sugar in their trolley which is leaving a trail on the floor, not realising that the person is, in fact, themselves. The distinguishing quality of De Se thought (for example De Se beliefs), is that it relates things to ourselves.

Pollock argues that without De Se beliefs the only beliefs someone could have are existential beliefs derived from sensations (such as that there is a table somewhere but not that there is a table before him). A person lacking De Se beliefs could not relate his environment to himself. He cannot even think of his body as his own without De Se beliefs. Lacking De Se beliefs means that he will not be able to combine existential beliefs into more elaborate beliefs. For example he would not be able to look at a table from various angles and thereby form an impression of its overall shape. Further, insofar as goals are conceived of as relative to the person who has them someone lacking a capacity for De Se beliefs could not formulate goals for themselves. According to Pollock, in order for De Se thought to be possible the agent must have a mental designator which is essentially a representation of the agent and this must be a logically primitive element on our system of mental representations.

Pollock asserts[95] that "consciousness of oneself as an entity consists in having De Se thought". He concludes from this that if something has a De Se designator amongst its mental designators then it can have De Se thoughts just like we can, so it could be conscious in precisely the same way as we are. Therefore he concludes:

There is no obstacle to building consciousness into an intelligent machine.[Pollock 1989, p.30]

The De Se designator is also invoked to explain how we re-identify other people. The idea goes like this: I remember that I (De Se designator), did such-and-such. That entails that I am the one who did such-and-such and enables me to re-identify myself as the person who did such-and-such. That, Pollock says, is all that there is to re-identifying myself. In the case of others it is only a matter of discovering generalizations about personal identity by considering our own cases and then applying those generalizations to others. The example he gives is that people can generally be re-identified in terms of their bodies.

With this account of the De Se designator Pollock believes that he has overcome the significant objections to regarding agents as material objects.

The rest of the discussion of agent materialism is taken up with a discussion of supervenient objects. Pollock gives as an example a statue which, he writes, supervenes on the lump of clay out of which it is made. The statue seems to have an identity separate from the lump of clay since by hollowing out the statue the clay can be made into a different lump of clay without the statue being made into a different statue. The statue supervenes upon both the lumps of clay. Another example he gives is of a house which he says supervenes upon a pile of bricks. Pollock says that people supervene upon their bodies and that this explains how it is that the body can change and even acquire prosthetic limbs yet the person remains the same. This however does not make persons in any way more remarkable objects than are houses or statues.

To summarise so far; both Pollock's arguments for token physicalism and for agent materialism amount to the claim that they seem plausible and that on his account they overcome the usual objections and counter-examples.

In chapter 3 Pollock argues for psychophysical supervenience on the basis of law-like functional properties of physical mental events. He writes that the principle of psychophysical supervenience claims that all mental states supervene on physical properties. He claims that to deny the principle of psychophysical supervenience is to insist that there is nothing physical that makes an occurrence a mental occurrence and nothing physical that endows a creature with mentality. This is to suppose that some physical occurrences just happen to be mental occurrences for no principled reason. That, he says,[96] is to endorse a kind of psychophysical magic which is beyond belief. Thus he believes token physicalism and agent materialism imply psychophysical supervenience. He writes:

> But to say that it is physical properties of a physical occurrence that make it a mental occurrence is just to say that mental states supervene on those physical properties. So any reasonable form of token physicalism or agent materialism seem to require psychophysical supervenience.[Pollock 1989, p.52]

Pollock follows this with a discussion of functional descriptions. He notes that the truth of law-like generalisations of the social sciences are dependent on structures and circumstances remaining constant. If structures or circumstances change sufficiently then these generalisations invariably fail. This he notes[97] is very damaging to functionalism as, in all its standard formulations functionalism requires there to be true generalisations. If there are no true generalizations then there are no functional properties, and thus no functionalism. To repair matters Pollock proposes that functional generalizations be hedged around with what amount to 'structure and circumstance remaining the same' clauses. These he spells out in some detail.[98]

Pollock spends the rest of this chapter discussing functionalist foundations for psychophysical laws. He points out that psychophysical supervenience results from laws relating mental states and physical properties. The kind of law he has in mind is one to the effect that a creature's having some physical property P nomically implies its being in some mental state M.[99] He insists that it is preposterous to suppose that what a creature is made of can have anything to do with what mental state it is in, except, indirectly, by influencing what structures can be built out of that stuff. He says it must be how it is made which is important. He illustrates this by saying that it does not matter if a can opener is made of steel or aluminium. (The sense in which persons are supposed to be in some way like can openers is not revealed.) Pollock concludes that insofar as mentality has a physical basis, it must reside in formal properties.[100]

The discussion continues with an analysis of the notion of a formal property. He concludes that formal properties comprise a continuum with static descriptions of the parts of an object at one end and functional properties at the other.[101] Static descriptions he characterises as making no reference to how the parts of what is described are shaped or arranged. He regards functional properties as the only plausible candidates, among formal properties, for providing a physical basis for mentality. He then writes:

> I assume, then, that it is the possession of a functional property that is at least causally (and perhaps logically) responsible for a cogniser's

being an a mental state.[Pollock 1989, p.64]

Having, in his own words, decided that "the physical half of a psychophysical nomic equivalence must be a functional property", he sets about sorting out what kind of functional property it might be. [102] This leads him to conclude that for a suitable functional theory T:

...the physical facts about a cogniser that make it the case that he is in a mental state M consist of his having a physical structure whose state can be put into a correspondence with mental states in such a way that their behaviour mirrors the behaviour of mental states (both realise T) and the cogniser is in that state of the structure that corresponds to M.[Pollock 1989, p.68]

Pollock next sets himself the task of describing the functional theory T that he has just deduced must exist. He writes:

I have argued that insofar as mentality has a physical basis, it must consist of mental properties being nomically equivalent to functional properties described by some purely psychological functional theory T. The theory T must be such that having a structure of a type characterised by T is nomically essential for the possession of the mental state M. If a cogniser currently has a structure of a type characterized by T, then his mental states conform to the generalisation comprising T. So T consists of generalisations whose current satisfaction is a necessary condition for being in M.[Pollock 1989, p.69]

His first step in describing T is to assume what he calls a rationality principle according to which, he says,[103] it is a necessary condition of mentality that a cogniser tends to be rational. He then discusses conditions that make it rational to be in a particular state and how being in some state contributes to the rationality or irrationality of other states or actions. He then preposes that the generalisations comprising T must be probabilistic generalisations to the effect that state-to-state transitions generally occur in accordance with the principle of rationality. This enables him to start to specify aspects of physical architecture for anything that has mind because, he says,[104] that a necessary condition for having any particular mental state is that the cognitive agent have a physical structure of some type S mimicking those aspects of rational architecture that govern that state.

Pollock moves on from this to consider counter-examples such as inverted spectra arguments and the population of China organised according to the functional specification (which he supposes to be possible), for his mind. (He contends that the Chinese nation thus organised would only have his mind if they were coerced in their actions by physical laws rather than acting out of free will. [105]) From this he moves to consider the physical basis for mental states (as distinct from mentality which he has just considered). He suggests [106] that what makes M a state of 'being appeared to redly' is that M is an appearance state where this generic kind has a physical basis described by the functionalist theory of mentality and that when one is in some appearance state, one is in M if and only of there is something red before one.

The rest of the chapter (chapter 4) is spent arguing that it is not possible for one person to know what qualia another person is experiencing, however it is possible to know such things as "my truck looks yellow to Jones". [107] This leads him to write:

> My conclusion is that all we can confirm about the mental states of other persons are the functional generalisations describing their rational architecture. Notice that if this is right, then there is no reason to regard human beings as interestingly different from suitably constructed non-human machines.[Pollock 1989, p.89]

In the remainder of the book Pollock considers what determines the content of a thought and what he calls cognitive carpentry. This consists of trying to specify what broad structural features a suitable functional theory must have in order to exhibit mentality.

Despite the fact that the book is written in a language that clearly assumes that any 'person machine' that is built will be a computer of some form, Pollock does not actually specify this. Nonetheless, I believe he would find my accounts of process and representation (in chapter 3 below), to be in conflict with his ideas. In chapters 4 and 5 (below,) I shall argue that the human form, including much of its detail, is crucial to our concept of a person. One consequence of this is that even if a functional description (any functional description), could be given of human beings this by itself would not make it possible to build a machine which would be a person. In chapter 7 (below,) I shall put forward criticisms of all functional theories which might be useful for attempts at person building.

All of these authors and indeed the whole computer metaphor seem to have been seduced by concepts handed down to them by traditional philosophy of mind. For all their protestations against dualism they are all concerned to preserve, one way or another, as much separation as they can between mental activity and physical activity. It is, in some ways, this that can make the computer metaphor seem attractive, for it appears to offer a way of understanding the same thing, namely

45

cognition, both as dependent on abstract properties and also, at the same time, as part of a causal sequence. Yet this kind of conceptual separation received its licence from and achieved its widespread acceptance through the account of dualism offered by Descartes; the very system that they are so concerned to avoid. (I do not, of course, want to say that dualism did not exist before Descartes, merely that he has been its most powerful exponent.) The kind of account of mind offered by Aristotle in which perception is both physical and mental and thinking and acting are bound in intimate relationship by such concepts as the practical syllogism is nowhere to be seen in the computer metaphor. I find this surprising. If one rejects dualism and then searches around in the history of western philosophy for an alternative, monist, account of mind the obvious starting point must be Aristotle. My critique and the ideas that I shall put forward however, are mainly influenced by the writings of Wittgenstein.

Notes

1.   Putnam 1987, pp.1-17.

2.   Putnam 1987, p.3.

3.   Putnam 1980, pp.70-84, *Do True Assertions Correspond to Reality?*

4.   By this I take him to mean is the image of the sentence under a mappping'.

5.   ibid. p.80.

6.   Putman 1980, pp.85-106, *Some Issues in the Theory of Grammer*, pp.106-131, *How to Talk About Meaning,* and p.269.

7.   Putnam 1987, Loc. Cit.

8.   Putman 1980, pp.429-441, *The Nature of Mental States.*

9.   ibid. pp.433-434.

10.   Putnam 1987, Loc. Cit.

11.   ibid. p2.

12.   ibid. p.2.

13.   ibid. p.2.

14.   Putman 1980, pp.85-106, *Some Issues in The Theory of Grammer.*

15.   Ex hypothesis it is effectively decidable whether any particular sentence of natural language is meaningful. In order to do this it must be possible to represent the meaningful sentence in the formal language, for any meaningful sentence conforms, by definition, to the grammatical rules of the language, and these are structural rules. By hypothesis, these rules can be represented in the formal language, and thus so can anything which has a structural pattern which can be formally deduced from

them, - such as a meaningful sentence.

16. Putnam 1987, Loc. Cit.
17. Putnam 1987, Loc. Cit.
18. Dennett 1969.
19. Dennett 1979.
20. Dennett 1987.
21. Ryle 1988.
22. Dennett 1969, pp.16-17.
23. ibid. p.18.
24. ibid. pp.19-32.
25. Quine 1960.
26. Dennett 1969, p.31.
27. ibid. p.39.
28. ibid. p.40.
29. Dennett 1979.
30. Dennett 1969, pp.16-17.
31. Dennett 1979, p.XVII.
32. Dennett 1969, p.39.
33. ibid. p.40.
34. ibid. p.30.
35. ibid. Chapter 1.
36. ibid. p.111.
37. ibid. p.112.
38. ibid. p.147.
39. ibid. p.156.
40. Dennett, 1979, *Brainstorms: Philosophical Essays on Mind and Psychology*.
41. ibid. p.XX.
42. ibid. p.122.
43. In some ways Dennett is in the business of breathing new life into the kinds of theory of mind held by Hume, Locke, and many others in whichmind is conceived of as containing distinct things (ideas, impressions, etc.) which are caused by and stand in some constant relation to things in the world. Fodor, whom I discuss below, also makes this observation. [144] The problems of infinite regress that are usually raised aagainst this kind oftheory are to be solved by the nesting of homunculi.
44. ibid. p.122.
45. ibid. pp.90-109.
46. Fodor, 1976, *The Language of Thought*.
47. Dennett, 1979, pp.119-122.
48. In a later paper in the same book (titled *Towards a cognitive theory of*

consciousness), Dennett recognises explicitly that there is more to be done and sets out to suggest how it might be accomplished. He comments that the picture of a human being as analogous to a large corporation is as old as Plato's Republic but that it seems to have this flaw: That it is not like anything to be such an organisation. An organisation lacks a soul. He writes:

> I prepose to construct a fully fledged I' out of sub-personal parts by exploiting the sub-personal notions of access already introduuced.[Dennett 1979, p.172]

This he goes on to attempt by presenting a flow chart diagram of a device that he suggests might be the kind of thing which would have a fully fledged I'. This consists of suitably interconnected perceptual analysers, problem solver blocks, speech act generators, and so forth. Dennett concludes by saying that all he is trying to do is to render immmplausible the charge that no entity describable solely by the resources of cognitive theory could posssibly seem to have an inner life.(See Dennett 1979, p.172.)

49.   Dennett, 1987, Styles of Representation' in *The Intentional Stance*.

50.   ibid. p.217.

51.   ibid. p.223.

52.   ibid. p.223.

53.   If the global definition of these roles includes the roles that the system's a*f*ctions play in the life of the society then this begins to look somewhat wittgensteinian.

54.   Dennett 1979, pp.119-122.

55.   Dennett 1969, p.39.

56.   ibid. p.40.

57.   Dennett 1987.

58.   Pylyshyn 1980, in *The Brain and Behavioural Sciences*.

59.   ibid. p.113.

60.   ibid. p.113.

61.   ibid. p.113.

62.   ibid. p.113, last paragraph.

63.   ibid. p.113, last paragraph.

64.   On this account, if this is not done semantics fail. Rules would cease to be semantically interpretable. These features must in turn be reflected in functional differences in the operation of the device. This, Pylyshyn writes, is what we mean when we say that the device represents something. Thus he concludes that all and only syntactically encoded aspects of the domain can affect the way a process behaves.

65.   Pylyshyn 1980, p.113, last paragraph.

66.   Pylyshyn 1980, p.112.

67.	ibid. p.114.
68.	ibid. p.114.
69.	ibid. p.114, in brackets.
70.	ibid. p.114.
71.	Fodor 1976.
72.	ibid. p.2.
73.	ibid. p.3.
74.	ibid. p.3.
75.	ibid. p.6.
76.	ibid. p.7.
77.	ibid. p.8.
78.	ibid. pp.19-22.
79.	ibid. p.31.
80.	ibid. p.74.
81.	Fodor 1981.
82.	ibid. pp.177-203.
83.	ibid. pp.197-198.
84.	ibid. p.202.
85.	Pollock 1989, *How To Build A Person: A Prologomenon*.
86.	Putnam 1961, Minds and Machines', in *Dimensions of Mind* Ed. by Sidney Hook.
87.	Pollock 1989, p.12.
88.	ibid. p.12.
89.	ibid. p.13.
90.	ibid. p.14.
91.	ibid. pp.15-16.
92.	ibid. pp.18-19.
93.	ibid. Chapter 2.
94.	ibid. p.22.
95.	ibid. p.29.
96.	ibid. p.52.
97.	ibid. p.55.
98.	ibid. pp.55-61.
99.	ibid. p.61.
100.	ibid. p.61.
101.	ibid. p.64.
102.	ibid. p.65.
103.	ibid. p.71.
104.	ibid. p.72.

105.   ibid. p.78.
106.   ibid. p.79.
107.   ibid. p.88.

3 A critique of the concepts of process and representation as used in the computer metaphor

In this chapter I shall be concerned to demonstrate that, in the sense that exponents of the computer metaphor use the words 'process' and 'representation', processes and representations are not usually characteristic of mind. This is not to deny that there are processes (including mental processes,) which are characteristic of mind. As Wittgenstein comments, hearing a tune or a pain growing greater or less are examples of mental processes[1] Rather, I want to emphasize that the word 'process' covers many diverse things and that the processing of a computer or its Central Processing Unit is one very specialised application of this word. A quote from Wittgenstein is apposite here:

> How does the philosophical problem about mental processes and states and about behaviourism arise? - The first step is the one that altogether escapes notice. We talk of processes and states and leave their nature undecided. Sometime perhaps we shall know more about them - we think. But that is just what commits us to a particular way of looking at the matter. For we have a definite concept of what it means to know a process better. (The decisive movement in the conjuring trick has been made, and it was the one that we thought quite innocent.) - And now the analogy which was to make us understand our thoughts falls to pieces. So we have to deny the yet uncomprehended process in the yet uncomprehended medium. And now it looks as if we had denied mental processes. And naturally we don't want to deny them.[Wittgenstein (Anscombe Trans.) 1981, §302]

What we need to clarify is the particular sense in which the operations of a computer are a process.

In the operation of a computer, at a most basic level, symbols, which are written, or stored, in one place, are erased, or moved, and written, or stored, in another place. This all goes forward under the control of a program. The result of all this usually takes the form of systematic manipulation of symbols. In consequence there is a controlled transformation from an earlier state to a later state via discrete intermediate steps.

All computers which might offer a route to person building conform to this pattern.

Let us now return to Dennett's claim about purposeful and diligent reasoning (discussed on page 18 above). He gives this as an example of a process. Dennett does not give what he regards as a paradigm case of purposeful and diligent reasoning, but perhaps working at and solving on paper a difficult calculation would be an example, or perhaps proving a mathematical theorem.

For Dennett, Putnam, Fodor and others, purposeful and diligent reasoning is a mental process, and what makes it true that such a process is going on is that the right kind of computer-like process was taking place in the brain. If, in fact, such a suitable process was not taking place in the brain then these authors are committed to saying that purposeful and diligent reasoning is not taking place. Thus, for these authors, the existence of this suitable computer-like process in the brain forms a crucial part of any conceptual analysis of purposeful and diligent reasoning. This seems to me to beg many questions.

Let us take calculating or doing a sum as an example of purposeful and diligent reasoning. The first question we might ask here is in virtue of what would we say, in everyday life, it is true that a person has calculated. The natural answer is that, amongst other things, he has got the right answer and can show how he arrived at his answer. Such simple facts are important:

We expect certain things of people who are doing a difficult calculation. We expect them, later on, to be able to demonstrate the steps of their reasoning, we expect them to concentrate hard, (and this can be seen in such things as objecting to extraneous distractions, showing signs of tiredness after having calculated, and so on,) and we expect them perhaps to make notes which are relevant to the calculation, and other such like things.

If sufficient of these kinds of things are not evident then we will be inclined to say that the person does not seem to be calculating, or that they find the calculation so easy as to need only to doodle, or that they are only pretending to calculate, or some similar thing. That is to say that being able to demonstrate the steps of their reasoning, having concentrated hard, having made notes, and similar such things are part of what we mean by 'having calculated', and that in the absence of these or suitable similar things we will have grounds for doubting that a person has indeed calculated. This arises from the nature of the concept of calculation: The concept of calculation (in this context), has no need of, and is not normally connected to anything to do with computer-like processes in the brain.

An enthusiast for the computer metaphor might object here that all this may be true, but what makes the result to be correct is that it and the steps of the calculation stand in a 1-1 relationship with certain states of the brain in the person who has calculated.

This also seems to me to be mistaken. What makes the result that this person arrives at correct is that he can demonstrate a practice of moving from one set of marks on paper (or suitable recording medium), to another, and that other people who are acknowledged as knowledgeable in this field will agree that he has followed the rules of transformation of these marks correctly. They will all agree when they give their judgments that this example is a correct application of the rules of arithmetic. That is what getting the right answer comes to. [2]

This might appear to be evidence of just the kind of inner processes that the computer metaphor enthusiasts claim goes on in the brain, but it is not. What makes it true that he has calculated, and thus a crucial part of what the calculation consists in, are those practices and activities (and other similarly relevant things), noted above. This is not to deny that this person calculated, simply it is to say that this is what we mean by calculation.

Let us now take the case of calculation in the head. This seems surely to be a paradigm case of an inner, mental, process which resembles the processing of a computer.

It is natural that if we ask someone who has done a calculation in their head for an introspective report that they will report that they, for example, found the prime factors, took the roots of those, and multiplied the results together. This is a description in terms which could be written on paper as a formal, written way of solving the problem. It is however unwarranted to suppose that because it can be expressed in this way that therefore there was a process going on in their brain which was formally equivalent, or even analogous, to that which could be written down on paper as the way to proceed from the problem to the solution.

What makes it true that he has done a calculation in his head and arrived at the correct answer and has found it difficult to do so will be his mental distraction while doing it, his having the right answer (the criterion of 'right' here being that competent persons can demonstrate this on paper), perhaps his mumbling to himself, perhaps walking up and down as he does it, perhaps his having been asked, or said he would, or in some other sense been expected to do the calculation, and so on. The things which make it true that he was doing a difficult calculation in his head are to be found in his actions in the context of his environment and circumstances. These things may not be necessary or sufficient conditions for the truth, they are most probably just a nexus of facts such that if sufficient hold then we will say that it is true.

These things, any of which, in a particular case, can be part of what doing a mental calculation consists in are things that together may go astray, bog down, leave us exhausted, and which take time - which is Dennett's description of a process - but they are not evidence of an inner, computer-like process. The idea of an inner computer-like process seems to me to arise from a mistaken picture of what is going in here. The thought seems to be that what is going on in mental calculation must be an analogue of what goes on when calculating on paper, and that because this can be shown to be equivalent to a large number of small, effectively computable, steps then what is going on in mental calculation must also be a large number of small steps. This line of thought gains most of its plausibility by completely ignoring the circumstances of these events. In order to be able to look distracted, to mumble to oneself, to walk up and down, and to be able to do any of the other things which go together to lead us to say that it is true that a person is doing a mental calculation a person needs to have a body and all the wherewithal (a face for expression, legs for walking, a social environment, etc.), to be a suitable subject to be described as walking up and down, mumbling, looking distracted, and any of the other things which might lead us to say that a person is concentrating hard.

These kinds of environmental circumstances quite literally are the kinds of things in virtue of which we say that someone is concentrating hard. It is from these circumstances that we know that the words are meant literally.

This can all be made much more clear if we consider the case of an alleged calculating parrot: We may say of a parrot that it mumbles, and the parrot may walk up and down, but if it should suddenly enunciate a mathematical theorem we will not be inclined to take all this as evidence of concentration. A parrot is the wrong kind of thing to be described as concentrating (in the normal non-metaphorical sense of the word). We might perhaps write a script for a film in which a parrot exhibited evidence of advanced mathematical abilities, however, if we were to do so, the script would need to contain detailed directions about people's reactions, murmurs of awe, hesitations, expressions of incredulity, and of looks in the parrot's eye, sage nods of its head and so on. In short, what would be needed in this film to make the idea of a parrot mathematical genius seem plausible would be a portrayal of large amounts of suitable environmental details. This, on a wittgensteinian view, is just what we would expect, for it is in virtue of such environmental details that such a thing would or would not be a parrot mathematical genius. The concept of a parrot mathematical genius requires such reactions from people who encounter such a thing. If a person was not astonished by a report of a parrot mathematical genius then he would not have grasped fully the concept of a parrot.

This is not, of course, to say that people cannot be deceived in such matters: If, in fact, the 'parrot' is a computer controlled mechanism in a parrot skin with a radio voice link, then, in fact, it is not a genuine parrot mathematical genius. Part of what we would mean by a genuine parrot mathematical genius is that it is a living parrot and does not contain a computer controlled mechanism or a radio voice link. Nonetheless people may be deceives by such a thing. Not all the contextual or environmental circumstances which go to make something true are always visible. Indeed in the case of a parrot mathematical genius many of them will be unremarked counter-factuals about the parrot such as If it were struck dumb then it would find some other means of 'communicating'.

For Putnam, Pylyshyn, and Fodor, the crucial matter is whether the parrot has the right kind of program running in its 'mental computer'. If it does, then it is a genuine mathematical genius.

Wittgenstein examines[3] an apparently paradigm case of mental process, namely making an effort to find the right expression for our thoughts while writing a letter. This does indeed seem to be a case of a computer-like mental process; that of putting something into words. Wittgenstein points out however, that this way of putting it is highly misleading, for it compares finding the right expression with translating into, or describing our thoughts in, words. If we think of actual cases we can see that this covers a multitude of diverse possibilities. It may be that I surrender to my mood and the expression comes, or that a picture occurs to me and I try to describe it, or an expression in a foreign language comes to me and I try to translate it, or that an onomatopoeic word occurs to me. All these would be examples of

55

what we call expressing our thoughts in words. In each case what is going on is clearly different. In surrendering to my mood what I write will be part of what being in that mood consists of (the mood is not some inner thing like a coloured cloud that I describe). If a picture occurs to me then what I write is more like an account of something I have remembered. (I treat with memories and mental imagery briefly below pages 71-72.) If an expression occurs to me in a foreign language then I am indeed translating something, but in this case what that comes to is attempting to express in english what the foreign phrase means to me. It is not clear until we examine the specific example whether this is a computer-like process or not. If an onomatopoeic word occurs to me then I may well be mumbling words as I write it playing with sounds and rhyme. (Whatever this may be, it is certainly not a clear example of a computer-like process.)

What these examples demonstrate is that the things we express by the phrase 'making an effort to find the right expression for our thoughts' are a heterogeneous bunch which may have no common characteristics other than being possible instances of ways in which we express our thoughts while writing a letter. Certainly they do not give grounds for supposing that there is really some computer like mental process going on in the person who is writing the letter which processes thoughts into verbal expressions. On the contrary, if the mind were like a computer then the heterogeneous nature of such examples would form problematic instances for the computer account. Some account would have to be given of how and why such diverse activities are in some sense 'the same'. This is not to say that a computer could not produce an equivalent performance to these activities, but it is to say that convincing grounds for believing that the mind is based on computer-like processes must be sought elsewhere.

Let us now move on to examine mental states (after all, computers are complex things with a huge variety of internal states). Perhaps mental states are simply very large classes of discrete brain states which are closely analogous to a computer's machine states (Fodor[4] thinks this).

To pursue this we need to look at some examples. Intending to move house is an example of a mental state. On the computer metaphor this could be understood as constantly being in one state of a very large class of machine states.

Such talk of machine states ignores the fact that what we mean by the mental state of intending to move house, and that in virtue of which it is true that someone is in such a mental state is that they do and display those things which are characteristic of intending to move house. For example, putting their current house on the market (getting an estate agent's valuation) or giving their landlord notice that they will quit, perhaps improving the garden for the estate agent's photographs but not bothering to re-tile the bathroom, perhaps starting to pack, or making enquiries about storage facilities, and so on. All these are the kinds of things which make it true that someone is in a mental state of intending to move house. This will be true whatever may be going on in their brain, (or any other part of their anatomy,) for these are the kinds of things we expect to be true when we say someone is intending to move house.

Of course the computer metaphor enthusiast may object that these kinds of behaviour individuate those machine states which constitute the mental state of intending to move house. Again, however, this reduces the computer metaphor to an implausible empirical claim which is in no way strengthened by cases such as this.

Let us look at another example of a mental state. Suppose I have bought a new, expensive, mountaineering jacket from a mail order firm and am hoping that it will arrive before the weekend. I might be described as being in the mental state of hoping the jacket will arrive. This state of hoping will consist in, amongst other things, my thoughts constantly returning to the subject, perhaps daydreaming about the jacket, perhaps looking up from my desk whenever there is a sound remotely like a postman, perhaps hurrying excitedly to the letter box when I return to the house and looking for a note saying that a parcel must be collected, perhaps explaining about the jacket if I am asked why I keep rushing to the letter box, and so on.[5]

The important point here is that it is in virtue of these kinds of things that it is true that I am hoping that my new jacket will arrive before the weekend, not in virtue of an inner process, computer-like or not. The same reply that I have raised before can also be raised here, and the answer is the same: If this behaviour is an external manifestation of an inner computer-like process then this is an empirical claim and the grounds for believing it must be found elsewhere.

It can be seen from this and the other cases I have examined why Fodor, (see page 29 above,) is mistaken in supposing that a Wittgensteinian or Rylean account reduces mental or psychological predicates to physical descriptions. None of the lists I have given of examples of behaviour which are part of what constitute a mental state or thought or some thinking have been exhaustive. I have deliberately used the locutions 'of this kind', and 'amongst other things', because the variety of environmental circumstances in which we may hope or have particular thoughts is effectively infinite. Mental predicates such

57

as hoping or thinking subsume all of them in their near infinity. There can be no question of an eliminative reduction. Analyses such as I have given are not the first steps to an eliminative reduction but a grounding of the abstract and mental in the physical and material. In this way the metaphysical dualism apparently implicit in mental attribution which Pylyshyn is so keen to avoid, can be seen to be illusory.

Next I want to examine what it might be on this account to hold an opinion. This might be described as a mental state. For the enthusiasts for the computer metaphor this will be to have a certain model of the world. For Putnam (discussed above pages 11-12,) this amounts to having a certain formal structure of symbols and mappings between them. Once again I want to examine specific examples.

Let us suppose that someone holds the opinion that a local tax is immoral. Again let us ask in virtue of what would we be disposed to say that someone holds this opinion. - Well perhaps they say so, and with feeling too. Probably they will express their opinion whenever the subject is discussed, possibly they will refuse to pay the tax. When the bill comes in the post they will open the letter with a certain kind of attention, perhaps intense interest, perhaps disdain, but not disinterest. (Possibly they will rip it up, think better of it, and ask the council for a copy.) Probably they will delay paying it until the last possible moment.

These are the kinds of things we would expect to find if it is indeed true that this person holds the opinion that that tax is immoral. No one of these conditions or dispositions will necessarily be true in all cases where someone holds that a particular tax is immoral, however if someone does indeed hold that a tax is immoral then we will expect that a large number of these and similar conditions would be found to be true. If it were found that a sufficient number of such indicative conditions were not true then we would be inclined to say that whatever this person may say he is probably indifferent to that tax.

It is a disposition to patterns of this kind of indicative behaviour that we mean when we say that someone holds an opinion that something is immoral. In consequence, whether or no a particular mapping or model of symbols could be found in the brain is neither here nor there. Such a thing cannot make it true that a person holds a particular opinion. At most it might be contingently true.

In general, from the cases we have examined, I can find nothing in our normal talk of mental states to encourage the belief that there must be a computer-like process which underlies or is needed to explain all or many cases of being in a particular mental state. If anything the cases I have examined would tend to subvert such a view.

Let us now turn to understanding as a possible source of examples to bolster up the computer metaphor. Wittgenstein makes many comments which are relevant to a conceptual analysis of 'understanding' while discussing related issues.[6] Amongst the points he makes is that the word 'understand' is used in an enormous variety of contexts and circumstances.

An apparently paradigm case of understanding which may seem to lend credence to the computer metaphor is that of being able to continue a series. (Wittgenstein discusses this at length.[7]) After all, the ability to continue a series correctly is certainly a test of whether the formula for the series has been understood, and writing the series down would seem to be done most naturally by calculating sequential values of the formula. Thus, in this case at least, understanding seems clearly to amount to performing, whether consciously or unconsciously, a calculation. This is surely a case of a mental process which would be most naturally understood as being performed by something, (possibly the brain), which is analogous to a computer in its functioning.

Wittgenstein asks us to imagine various cases.[8] Suppose one person writes down a series of numbers with a second person watching him and tries to find the law or formula by which the first arrives at each of the succeeding terms of the sequence. Suddenly the second person exclaims "Now I can go on!" and he does so correctly. He has understood. This understanding made its appearance in a moment. This is not typically characteristic of a process.

Perhaps, one might suppose, the second person had been performing a mental process of trying various algebraic formulae in turn against the terms of the sequence that were written down. This is certainly possible, but even if someone gives this as an introspective report of how they arrived at the formula by which the terms of the sequence are generated, we have seen above, while considering mental calculations, that what doing a mental calculation comes to is crucially dependant on environmental facts and circumstances and not on internal the functioning of the person. Consequently, even if it is true that some such mental process accompanied the understanding, it is not in virtue of this that it is true that he has understood.

For an example of this kind it is also important that we can imagine many other ways in which the person watching might come to understand how to generate the series. Perhaps he watches with a feeling of tension and many vague thoughts going through his head. Suddenly he asks himself what is the series of differences, and he finds the series 2, 4, 6, 8, 10.... Now he says he can go on. He has understood.

This bares little resemblance to a process on a computer. To construe the vague thoughts as a process does not help at all. It might well have been the vague thoughts running through his head which were distracting his attention and only when they got bogged down and he turned his full attention to the problem did he understand. Again the vague thoughts might have been remembering that once, while waiting for a friend at the end of a class at school, he had overheard another pupil discussing just this series with the teacher.

Another possibility is that he looks at the series and says "I know that series" and proceeds to write down the continuation. Perhaps he has recognised it as one he has worked with before. This is nothing like a process.

Perhaps he says nothing and simply continues the series.

None of these examples give any encouragement to the view of mind as analogous to a computer performing a process. None of them clearly display features which are characteristic of computer processes.

Wittgenstein points out[9] that understanding the principle of a series must mean more than that the formula for the series occurs to us. It is quite imaginable that the formula should occur to someone and that nevertheless he should not understand. What justifies us in saying that he understands are the circumstances of his knowing how to go on.

We also talk of understanding a word or a phrase. This does not sound much like a process, but could it perhaps be some kind of a mental state analogous to the machine state of a computer? Wittgenstein points out[10] that depression, excitement, and pain, are typical of what we call mental states, however these words behave differently to 'understanding'. We may talk of someone being depressed the whole day, or of being in greatly excited all day, or of being in continuous pain for days, but can one talk of understanding continuously in the same sense? "He has understood this word since yesterday." makes sense. If I now say "He has understood this word continuously since yesterday." what has been added to the meaning? In the sense in which one can be continuously depressed such a sentence is nonsense.

An enthusiast for the computer metaphor might object here that the analysis I have given is too simplistic. The line might run something like this:

Of course this is an empirical hypothesis, of course it remains to be demonstrated, this is simply a consequence of computers being a relatively recent invention. Our language and concepts will change as these things are demonstrated. The computational aspect of mind lies buried at a deeper level. We are able to mean words and it is this that determines what they mean, not their context. Context may sometimes confuse an audience but it does not change what the speaker meant. The meaning is internal to him, and for this to be possible in all the variety of circumstances in which a word may be used is clear evidence of some kind of record or representation of the correct use of the word which is internal to the speaker. What we mean when we say that someone has understood is that they have got their internal representations right. It is from reflection on how such representations can get expression that we deduce that there must be some kind of process involved. This combination of representation and process leads naturally to the computer metaphor.

This position or something like it, seems quite a natural one to me. It consists of two parts. The first is an empirical claim (which is made no more plausible by an explanation that our language will change if it is found to be true). The second is more serious and amounts to the claim that there must be representations for it to be possible to mean things and that this is what is exhibited in understanding.

To me it seems that our language lends itself very naturally to this way of talking. For example, we ask people 'Do you really mean that?' when seeking confirmation that we have understood them correctly and sometimes we talk of words and images being meaningful when they seem to have a coercive force of their own.

Wittgenstein treats with these kinds of cases as part of a broader theme.[11] First he draws our attention to the way we use, ('the grammar of') 'to fit', 'to be able', and 'to understand'. He asks us to reflect on when a cylinder C is said to fit into a hollow cylinder H. To me it seems that the answer depends on the circumstances in which we are using these words. For some applications, (e.g. some types of wooden building blocks for children,) we will say that C fits into H if the end of C can be jammed rigidly into H. For other applications, (e.g. passing cable down a pipe,) we will say C fits into H only if C can be passed easily right the way through H. For yet other application, (e.g. the fit of a bearing into its sleeve in an engine,) we will require that C fit inside H but be only a tiny amount smaller than H. In different circumstances the words 'to fit' are used differently.

Wittgenstein then asks us to consider under what circumstances we would say that C ceased to fit into H at a particular time. In the case of the children's building blocks, if we find one day that they will no longer fit together, we will probably look for an explanation. Let us suppose that we find that the blocks are made of wood and have changed their shape as a consequence of getting wet. Then we would be inclined to say that they ceased to fit when they got wet. The criteria here for the change having taken place at a particular time is the fact that they got wet at a certain time understood in the context of a presumed causal connection between their getting wet and the change of shape. In the case of passing a cable through a pipe it might be that the manufacturer has changed the specification of the cable (say cable type A), and that type A is no longer sufficiently flexible to pass round the angles of the bends which are typical of the pipes through which it must be threaded. It would then make sense to say that type A cable ceased to fit through such pipes about six months ago. The criteria would be that this drum of cable type A does not fit through the pipes today and that it has taken about six months to get from the manufacturer to this first instance of its not fitting.

In the case of the bearing sleeve in an engine one might say that it used to fit about five hundred miles ago. The criteria for this is that in repairing the engine today the mechanic has found that the sleeve is worn and judges that it has been unacceptably worn for about the last five hundred miles over which the car has been driven.

These examples seem to me to demonstrate clearly how complicated criteria of correct application of 'fitting' can be. The notion of fit, at least in these examples, is a mechanical notion to do with physical bodies, one might therefore expect the criteria of its application to be relatively simple. In fact, as we can see, they are not. The intuitive idea that meaning is some internal quality of the speaker which he can somehow 'do' seems, from these examples, unlikely, for what could be common or 'the same' for all cases of fitting?

The potential for complexity with criteria for the correct use of 'understanding', and for saying when someone began and ceased to understand will be at least as great. In the case of continuing (and therefore understanding), the series that we considered earlier Wittgenstein points out[12] that "Now I can go on." seems to mean much the same thing as "Now the formula has occurred to me.", but in general with understanding this is not so. Each case of understanding could be quite different.

Despite observations of these kinds the sense or image of meaning being somehow internal seems to force itself upon us. The meaning of a word seems to be in that word and, since we utter these words, in us. It seems sometimes to be very difficult to believe that what we mean by saying that someone is calculating in their head is a collection of environmental facts and behavioural dispositions any of which could, in principle, be observed if circumstances were right. Language in this way has a coercive quality. One almost cannot help thinking of mental calculation as an inner, private, activity which takes place in one's mind, (quite possibly literally in one's head).

Wittgenstein treats with this also. He is concerned to note that there is no totality of conditions for any particular case such that, if they were all fulfilled then the word would indeed find its application. If there were such a totality, then by fulfilling all the criteria of application in a particular case we could send someone for a walk, which we clearly can not. His point is that in each case of the application of a word or a rule, a new judgement is needed for it to find its application in that particular case.

Let us apply this to the case of writing out the terms of a series (say, start with 1 and add 2). Here we seem to have a paradigm case of something in which all the terms are determined in advance. It is as if by meaning them we somehow in our thoughts range over the whole series, right to infinity. This would seem to constitute a counter-example to the idea that in writing each term of the series a new judgement is needed.

The force of this counter-example wanes somewhat when one asks if it might not be that a pupil in writing out this series writes 1, 3, 5, 7,...999, 1003, 1005, 1007, 1009,...(omitting 1001). When we point this out to the pupil he doesn't understand our criticism and replies, "But that's how you meant me to do it". He then points to the series where we say he has made an error and says, "I just went on the same way". In such a case there would be nothing amongst the previous examples that we had shown him to which we might point and give as explanation as to why he is wrong. It might be that it just comes naturally to him to continue the series in this way.

There is, of course, a sense in which one might say that when we asked the pupil to write the series formed by beginning with 1 and adding 2, we knew that we meant him to write 999, 1001, 1003,..... This, however, is only to say that, if, when we instructed him to write the series, someone had asked us what we would write after 999 if we were writing that series, we would have replied 1001, 1003,... etc. This tells us about how we would be disposed to act in particular circumstances, not about something that was in some occult way contained in our meaning of the series. The way in which the algebraic formula for the series can be said to determine the series is only the way we take the algebraic formula as determining our dispositions to act. If we feel that the algebraic formula coerces precisely what we shall write that is because we are very strict in our judgements as to what is, or what is not, acceptable as an expansion of the formula. (It is not as if there is no leeway in our judgements. The formula is not supposed to determine the script in which the terms are written down or the quality of the paper on which it is written.)

Wittgenstein suggests[13] that we get into this kind of confusion because we have a picture of how the expansion must go which is analogous to how a machine must move. It can seem (with a car engine, for example), that all future movements are determined in advance in some way in the machine, as if the parts could move only in that way and no other. This is because we forget the possibility of their bending, breaking off, melting, distorting, and so on. It is as if we think of the future movements of the machine as being definite in the way that objects lying in a draw waiting to be taken out are definite. This is to treat the machine as a symbol of its future movements, and of course the movements of the machine-as-symbol are indeed already determined. They are determined by us in our application of whatever rules we may have for deriving the future movements of the machine-as-symbol.

To return then to our question of how the meaning of a word or a phrase can be 'in' the word, how really meaning it can somehow determine its meaning more certainly, the answer is now clear. Words and phrases do not exist in isolation. There could not be one, and only one, occasion on which a report was given, a calculation was made, a rule was followed, an order given, a letter written, an alarm was shouted, a taxi was hailed, an apology was offered, a greeting was given, or any of the other things we do with words and phrases. These things, and things like them, playing chess, competing in sports, falling in love, going to parties and so forth are customs, uses, and institutions. We learn our daily language in a society, perhaps large, perhaps small, of language users. In consequence we will have lived, (and most of us continue to live,) in a sea of such customs, uses, and institutions, and it is as a part of these that words and phrases have their uses and find their meanings. To say that we mean a word is only to say that if we were asked some question about how people should react to it, what its role is, what kind of response to it is required, we should be disposed to answer in some way which was definite at the time we uttered it. We utter our words and indulge in our uses, customs, and practices with some expectation of the effects they will have. (Even if we sing in the bath under the impression that no one will hear us, that is itself an expectation about the effect of the words.) Other people speak our language also. They too will have expectations, they too will share in our customs, uses, and practices. We cannot flout their expectations about the words of our language, and the customs, uses, and practices of our society and still hope to be understood. In any case of uttering words or phrases, or taking part in the customs, uses, or practices of a society there are rules which must be followed and which are governed by the expectations of others, however, as each instance of the use of a word or participation in a practice is different, there is also room for the exercise of judgement. Each time we speak or interact socially we exercise a rule and also, extend that rule to an instance that it has never covered before.[14]

As Wittgenstein puts it:

> To understand a language is to be master of a technique.[Wittgenstein (Anscombe Trans.), 1981, §109]

Meaning does not require internal representations, and the examples that we have examined show no signs of them. Understanding does not require the concepts of process or representations for its elucidation. Wittgenstein seems to me to put the matter well when he writes:

> Try not to think of understanding as a mental process at all. - For that is the expression which confuses you. But ask yourself: In what sort of case, in what kind of circumstances, do we say "Now I know how to go on"...
>
> In the sense in which there are processes (including mental processes) which are characteristic of understanding, understanding is not a mental process.[Wittgenstein (Anscombe Trans.) 1981, §154]

I believe that Wittgenstein's explanation of continuing a series accounts for our intuitive sense of being able to 'really mean' something (noted above page 63). It also meets Dennett's concerns (discussed above on pages 15-16,) about the limits of extensional, truth functional logic, and the implications of intensionality. This account of meaning is not grounded in extensional logic but in the role that language plays in our lives, and the way the world is. (I shall have more to say about this in chapters 4 and 5 below.) This also makes quite clear why Fodor is mistaken to suppose that Wittgenstein is in the business of supplying an eliminative reduction of psychological predicates to behavioural predicates (discussed pages 29-31, above).

In brief, I do not believe that computer-like processes are characteristic of mind because a close consideration of abilities and attributes that are characteristic of mind show no sign of them and reveal no need for them in order to explain those aspects of mind.

Two

Let us now turn to the hypothesis of representations and apply it to knowing and knowledge: Knowledge is often cited as a paradigm example of a mental attribute which requires the hypothesis of mental representation for its elucidation. For Putnam the idea that knowing something involves having formal, structural, internal representations is central to his view of mind. Dennett, (above page 20,) is more subtle and writes of explicit, implicit, and tacit representations. How much of his account would remain intact if explicit and implicit representations were shown to be unnecessary for an understanding of mind in all but a few specialized cases, is not completely clear to me, but I think not very much. Certainly the Content and Consciousness account of mind would collapse as would the Brainstorms account. Whatever the case, it will be my case that what Dennett calls explicit and implicit representations are unnecessary for an account of mind. Pylyshyn is so closely committed to the computer metaphor that without representations he would have nothing to say about mind. His interest seems to be in computers and through the metaphor, almost incidentally, in mind. Fodor, while he may have a wider perspective, has put all his goods in one boat, namely the computer metaphor. Pollock is irrevocably committed to functionalism.

Wittgenstein, as usual, asks us to consider when we use the term 'knowledge' or say someone knows something. There seem to be considerable differences between the sense of 'know' in different cases. For example, 'I know that Paris is bigger than Vienna', 'I know the alphabet', 'I know Joe Bloggs', 'I know I had my keys this morning; now what did I do with them?', and 'Now I know!'. These are all natural everyday uses of the word, in addition, for the purposes of this essay, we may note that there are uses which are confined mainly to philosophers such as 'I know the earth existed for some time before I was born,' or 'I know I have two hands'.

As before, I now want to ask when such assertions would be justified. When would I be justified in saying that I know that Paris is bigger than Vienna? What would make it true that I know ?

One answer to this is, of course, many and different things which will vary with 'circumstances'. If we imagine a pupil answering questions in an exam then the principal criterion will be that he writes down the correct answer. This requires him, amongst other things, to understand the practice of sitting examinations, and to be able to read the questions as well as to be able to give the correct answer. If any of these things are lacking however he will not be able to answer the question correctly. In such circumstances a pupil would be judged not to know that Paris is bigger than Vienna.

In other circumstances, perhaps the pupil can assert that Paris is bigger than Vienna, we will say that he knows it. This, however, would seem to exclude a mute from such knowledge. Perhaps we should say that someone knows it if they can indicate this knowledge in some appropriate form. This is now so vague as to make the representations hypothesis seem attractive

Such a train of thought seems to support Putnam and the representations hypothesis. It does so because we have become confused. A pigeon in a psychology laboratory can learn to indicate that 'Paris is bigger than Vienna' by pecking the appropriate buttons. The similarity only arises because we have lost sight of the context of this knowing. If the pupil in the exam turns out not to know that as a consequence of Paris being bigger than Vienna it will have more people, or more houses, or cover a larger area, or if we find that this pupil has no idea what a city is, or that Paris and Vienna are places (suppose he thinks they are species of iced buns), or suppose that he is referring to two dogs which are named Paris and Vienna, then, in the sense in which we meant the word we will say that this pupil does not know that Paris is bigger than Vienna.

'I know', in this case, is part of a much wider web of abilities, practices and techniques. We would only be willing to say of someone that they indeed know that Paris is bigger than Vienna if they also know sufficient of the relevant conceptually connected facts. For example, we would expect someone who knows that Paris is bigger than Vienna also to know what it is to be bigger than, what places are, what cities are, and so on. Facts, concepts, practices, techniques, and abilities of this kind which we expect someone to know in virtue of their knowing that Paris is bigger than Vienna are, I want to say, conceptually connected to knowing that Paris is bigger than Vienna.

These conceptually connected facts, concepts, practices, techniques, and abilities may or may not be individually crucial to our willingness to attribute knowledge that Paris is bigger than Vienna to someone. Which, if any, of these conceptually connected facts, concepts, practices, techniques and abilities are crucial may even vary between individual speakers of our language. For example, most English speakers would probably agree that someone who did not know what a city was could at best have only a very limited understanding of 'Paris is bigger than Vienna'. On the other hand, while we might expect someone who knew that Paris is bigger than Vienna also to know where Paris and Vienna are situated, most English speakers would be unlikely to conclude that they did not truly know that Paris is bigger than Vienna if they should find that the person did not know where these cities are situated, however, some English speakers in some circumstances would so conclude. (Perhaps they are pedantic teachers of geography.) What seems certain is that if, on interrogation, we were to find that someone who purported to know that Paris is bigger than Vienna was ignorant or lacking in sufficient of the conceptually connected facts, concepts, practices, techniques, and abilities then any English speaker would conclude that that person did not know that Paris is bigger than Vienna. Exactly which or how many of the conceptually connected facts, concepts, practices, techniques, and abilities would need to be lacking before an English speaker would be prone to say that that person did not know that Paris is bigger than Vienna despite his assertion to the contrary will vary between English speakers. What is important here is simply that if sufficient of the conceptually connected facts, concepts, practices, techniques, and abilities are lacking then that person cannot know what they say they know despite their assertions to the contrary. This is a feature of the nature of meaning in language.

Each of the facts, practices, techniques, and abilities which are conceptually connected to knowing that Paris is bigger than Vienna will itself be conceptually connected to other facts, concepts, practices, techniques, and abilities in a similar fashion. Ultimately these chains of conceptual connections can be terminated and thus grounded in capacities for action, abilities, and bodily powers.

For example, a grasp of the concept 'bigger than' rests crucially on an ability to distinguish an object which, in context, is 'bigger than' from one which is 'smaller than' another. Such an ability will depend crucially in turn on the possession of appropriate 'bodily powers', for example, the power to indicate and the power to discriminate size. That is to say that if someone or something is quite unable to discriminate which of two (relevantly similar,) objects is the bigger of the two and which the smaller and is also quite unable to indicate in any way which of the two is being referred to as 'the bigger' and which as 'the smaller' then we will be unable to ascribe a grasp of the concept 'bigger than' to it in the ordinary sense of the word no matter what assertions are made to the contrary. The concept 'bigger than' simply does not get application in such a case. (An ordinary computer without appropriate transducers and actuators can do neither of these things.)

Thus a close consideration of Putnam's own example provides no evidence at all for mental representations (in his specialized sense of models and 1-1 correspondences). What makes it true that the pupil knows that Paris is bigger than Vienna are the kinds of further abilities, practices, and knowledge that we have been considering above. This remains true as an analysis of our concepts whatever the case with representations.

As usual, with such claims, it would be possible for Putnam to retreat to a position of a purely empirical hypothesis: Thus he might claim that in fact representations form a crucial part of the mechanism by which such powers and abilities function. If this is so then this example provides no evidence for it.

For D.C. Dennett my critique of this example is less damaging in that he could appeal to tacit representations as the kind of thing which accounts for bodily abilities and powers, and thus maintain that representations are indeed necessary for a successful explanation of mind. This may be true, but naming such things as tacit representations does not explain them, and Dennett has not spelled out how tacit representations fit into standard computer theory.

For knowledge of this kind the matter is well summed up by Wittgenstein when he writes:

> 'I know' often means: I have proper grounds for my statement. So if the other person is acquainted with the language game, he would admit that I know.[Wittgenstein (Paul & Anscombe Trans.) 1974, §18]

The second of the examples I listed above was of knowing the alphabet. If one asks 'When does someone know the alphabet?' the answer is presumably all the time. Many people really could repeat the alphabet in their sleep, however, this is not, by itself, enough for us to say that someone knows the alphabet. A tape recorder doesn't know the alphabet at all, whatever may be recorded on the tape. What makes it true that I know the alphabet is that I can use it to look up words in a dictionary, can repeat it, can write the letters, can read them as individual characters, and so on. In this way, knowing the alphabet is clearly similar to knowing that Paris is bigger than Vienna.

There are however also differences between knowing the alphabet and knowing that Paris is bigger than Vienna: That Paris is bigger than Vienna is something we easily forget, for which we might have to try hard to remember when the information is needed, and for most people for most of the time is not a vitally important fact. It sounds queer to say that I know Paris is bigger than Vienna when I am asleep. In contrast to this, most literate people would find it difficult to imagine themselves forgetting the alphabet. If it should transpire that someone does indeed not know the alphabet then we will probably suspect that they have a lesser mastery of reading, writing, and spelling than they would have if they could recite the alphabet. (That these skills may in fact be quite separable in no way alters this conceptual analysis.) For most of us, knowing the alphabet forms an important part of what we expect when we believe that a person can read, write, or spell.

These differences are differences in the grammar of 'know' in these two circumstances. The alphabet is something usually known by rote whereas the fact that Paris is bigger than Vienna is not. (The question 'When do we know something?', is itself a puzzle which would rarely be raised outside of philosophy. I use it here as a tool for investigating grammar.) Both these examples of knowing involve mastery of a technique, but whereas one technique seems to be crucial to a wide range of skills which are important in our daily lives, the other is not.

In both these cases the grammar of 'knows' shows a close kinship with that of 'can' and 'to be able'. None of this lends any credence to the internal representations hypothesis.

This sense of 'know' which is similar to 'can' and 'to be able' is also at work in cases in which we have a sudden insight or understanding and exclaim 'Now I know!'. This might be a case of seeing the solution to a puzzle, or finding confirmation of a suspicion after much searching. In the case of a puzzle the kind of thing that will make it true that they do indeed know will be such things as being able successfully to solve the puzzle, or to explain the successful solution to a puzzle. In the case of finding a suspicion justified we will expect that, amongst other things, that a person acquainted with this language game would also agree that he knows. In such a case 'Now I know' is closely akin to 'Now I can demonstrate this to somebody else'.

By the very nature of its grammar, being akin to 'to be able', these uses of 'know' do not suggest internal representations. It is only once the idea of knowledge as some kind of internal object has received some support and become regarded as in some way the normal form of explanation of human abilities that internal representations come to seem an appropriate tool for any attempt to elucidate or give explanations about human abilities. Indeed the suddenness with which we may come to know the solution to a puzzle or with which 'the penny may drop' or our suspicions harden into a conviction would seem at first sight to argue against internal representations of Putnam's kind or of the kind that Dennett calls 'explicit' or 'implicit'. [15]

As ever the computer metaphor enthusiast may retreat to an empirical claim, and as ever they must seek justification for it elsewhere.

Another example of the use of the word 'know' is in the exclamation

'I know I had it this morning!'. (Let us suppose that someone has lost their car keys and exclaims thus.) Putnam would say that the person's inner representations form a model of the way the world was that morning and that if, in reality, he did indeed have the keys that morning then his statement is true and they do know, and if he did not then the statement is false.

We can imagine various contexts to go with such an exclamation: Perhaps the person has had them in their pocket the whole time. Perhaps he could not have had them because someone else was using them to drive the car that morning. Perhaps the person is disputing whether someone else could have been driving the car that morning.

The kinds of thing which we will expect if this statement is true are that it is possible for the person to have had the keys that morning (for example that such car keys exist and that that morning's circumstances admit of the possibility of them being in that person's possession that morning). We will also expect that the person's circumstances make it possible that they could have been in possession of them that morning. (For example that they had the opportunity.) In this case one of the things that will lead us to believe that it is true that this person had their car keys that morning is that they are able to tell us a detailed story of what they did that morning and how the car keys came into it. In such a case we know that if they did not have the keys then the story must be false. (This lends weight to the first assertion because while we might not be surprised if a person is mistaken about whether he had the car keys that morning, we do not expect them to elaborate a whole story which is false.)

It is in virtue of such things as these that we will judge it true or false that a person had the car keys that morning, for these things are part of what we mean by having the car keys that morning. This remains true whether there are internal representations or not. Once more, the internal representations hypothesis can be seen to be an empirical hypothesis which, if it is true, must seek its justification elsewhere. This case of knowing lends no weight to it.

Finally, in this treatment of knowing, let us examine the specialist philosophical uses of 'know' as in 'I know the earth existed before my birth'. Such uses and criticisms of these uses normally form part of a study of scepticism. I am not concerned here with scepticism, however, Wittgenstein's comments on the subject seem to me to shed some light on more general aspects of what we mean by 'know'.

Wittgenstein points out[16] that there are ways in which we can use 'know' in connection with memory which are not statements about facts and abilities but are like ground rules by means of which the rest of our lives are made able to proceed. In On Certainty[17] he asks what I am remembering when I say that I have had a bath everyday for the last month. Clearly I do not remember each day and each particular bath. What I know is that I bathed each day. I do not need to derive this in order to say I know it. Equally, I may say 'I felt a pain in my arm'. This does not suggest that the location of the pain came into consciousness; certainly the location of the pain need not come into consciousness as I say this.

For both these cases, on Putnam's account, it would be necessary that the knowledge of the pain without specific location, and the fact of having taken daily baths without specifically remembering the occasions would have to be explicitly represented. More generally, any 'piece' of information, such as the fact that Paris is bigger than Vienna may be expressed in a very large number of ways each of which appears to need a separate representation. For example, 'Paris has a larger area than Vienna', 'Paris has a larger population than Vienna', 'it is further from one side of Paris to the other than it is from one side of Vienna to the other', and so on. If Putnam is correct this points to each new fact represented giving rise to an explosive increase in the number of representations that the mind contains.

Computer metaphor enthusiasts often take the line that all these facts are computed from a few basic facts. This, once again, flies in the face of experience, There is no obvious sense in which we compute something like 'Paris has a larger area than Vienna' prior to each occasion of our exhibiting knowledge of it. Once more the computer metaphor must admit itself forced back upon an empirical hypothesis which lacks evidence or justification.

Wittgenstein points out that such propositions as 'I have never been in Asia minor,' and 'I know that I am now in England', are propositions which, were they to prove false, would topple all my other judgements as they fell. To be wrong about this might be akin to coming to believe that I am mad. For if I could be wrong about this, it seems that I might be wrong about anything. He writes:

> Our knowledge forms an enormous system. And only within this system has a particular bit the value we give it.[Wittgenstein (Paul & Anscombe Trans.) 1974, §410]

Propositions of the kind 'I know I have never been in Asia minor', are like foundations for our system of knowledge. They are not paradigm cases of knowing and are usually used only by philosophers. Propositions such as 'I know that the earth existed for some time before my birth', are more fundamental still. If this were false, then it seems

72

that anything at all might be false. Wittgenstein describes propositions like these as the river bed of our thought. They are that upon which the flow of our thought rests. Nonetheless, rivers do shift their beds, sometimes overnight. If this were to happen then our world would have undergone a catastrophic collapse. (This would perhaps be what the sudden, unexpected, and total defeat of a civilisation in war by an alien culture would be like for the inhabitants. Overnight everything, including their most basic values could be changed.)

In the light of what I have written, it seems worth asking how the notion of knowledge as representations arises, for it seems a very natural one which almost presents itself to us. It is certainly older than the computer metaphor. Dennett[18] ascribes it to the entire empiricist tradition.

It seems natural to suppose that in part it is suggested by a comparison between mental imagery and pictures. Mental images can seem like pictures and also to be something that is clearly 'in the mind'. If one accepts this then it is easy to suppose that the mind contains some representations as pictures. This model is quickly collapsed:

For most people the images that they have when they imagine a tiger does not have a definite number of stripes. The number of stripes can be decided by activities such as drawing it. It is also quite easy to demonstrate that if someone can imagine the word 'university' written clearly then if they read the letters that they see in their imagination both forward and backwards the times that they take to do so are close to those they take when spelling the word backwards and forwards from memory. The times are not close to those they take in spelling the word when it is written in front of them. Whatever mental images may be, one falls rapidly into confusion if one supposes them to be like pictures.

Wittgenstein suggests another source of the representations fable: The similarity between the grammar of 'to know' and 'to see'. He writes:

'I know' has a primitive meaning similar to and related to 'I see' ('wissen', 'videre'). And 'I knew he was in the room, but he wasn't in the room' is like 'I saw him in the room, but he wasn't there'. 'I know' is supposed to express a relation, not between me and the sense of a proposition (like 'I believe') but between me and a fact. So that the fact is taken into my consciousness.... This would give us a picture of knowing as the perception of an outer event through visual rays which project it as it is onto the eye and the consciousness. Only the question at once arises whether one can be certain of this projection. And this picture does indeed show how our imagination presents knowledge, but not what lies at the bottom of the presentation. [Wittgenstein (Paul & Anscombe Trans.) 1974, §90. His emphasis]

Knowledge and knowing facts would seem to be the computer metaphor's strongest ground, for these appear to be entirely in the mind and to be composed of discrete bits, yet, as we have seen, there is no sign in our normal or common instances of knowing things of anything like process or representations of a form which might encourage us to a belief in the computer metaphor. For other areas of our mental life such as hoping, fearing, loving, feeling sad, feeling glad, being joyful or depressed, appreciating beauty, standing in awe, empathizing, engaging in moral struggle, striving for a better world, and so on, the case for the computer metaphor is even less substantial.

This bodes ill for any project to build a person: I noted above (page 6) that the computer metaphor without representations collapses into primitive behaviourism and that any optimism that a person might one day be built rests on the computer metaphor (page above 6). Yet what I have just shown is that even in what would usually be considered paradigm cases of computer-like mental events there is no trace of computer-like processes or representations. If the prime examples of mental life which were to be explained by the computer metaphor show no sign of computation then there seems to be little rational ground for the belief that the mind is significantly and relevantly like a computer. At best, the belief is an empirical hypothesis which lacks any substantial evidence.

What I take myself to have shown is that in many cases of mental attributes that one would expect to form exemplars of mental attributes which are suitable for explanation by the computer metaphor, such as calculating on paper, calculating in the head, intending to move house, or hoping a parcel will arrive in the post, there is no sign of computer-like representations or processes. This suggests that the computer metaphor is irrelevant to any interesting answer to the question 'What is mind?'.

In order for it to be true that computer-like representations or processes were relevant for our understanding of what mind is it would have to be shown that our concepts of paradigm mental attributes such as intending, hoping, fearing, calculating, and so forth required these concepts for their explanation or elucidation. In particular it would have to be shown that they were necessarily drawn into any answer that might be given to questions such as 'What makes it true that John is intending?' or 'What makes it true that John is afraid?', and so on.

I believe that it is clear from the considerations put forward in this chapter that computer-like processes and representations are irrelevant to an elucidation of our everyday concepts of 'intending', 'calculating', 'understanding', and other mental attributes. It therefore seems that the only fashion in which computer-like representations and processes might be relevant to an elucidation of the nature of mind would be if they are drawn into such an account as an hypothesis that would be causally necessary for mind to be possible. This, which it would seem could only be an empirical hypothesis, has not been demonstrated. In the next two chapters I shall show that other sets of bodily circumstances are conceptually necessary for us to be able to ascribe many common attributes of mind (at least they are necessary if the words are used in their everyday senses), and that the history of a thing is crucial to whether it is a person. Since, as will become clear, these circumstances cannot be analysed in terms of the computer metaphor, this will demonstrate that the computer metaphor is inadequate to answer questions of the form 'What is intention?', 'What is mind?', and similar things, and that it can only be as an empirical hypothesis that it has any relevance to these questions at all.

These observations, if correct, not only show that the computer metaphor is almost certain not to provide a route to person building but also that systems of explanation based on the computational view of mind, such as cognitive psychology, are most unlikely to yield interesting answers to questions such as 'What is mind?'

Notes

1.   Wittgenstein (Anscombe Trans.) 1981.

2.   The rules in question will not, of course, be completely arbitrary. They are founded in such practical problems as successfully constructing bridges that will stay up, building aircraft, and other similar things.

3.   ibid. §335.

4.   Fodor 1981, pp.170 et seq.

5 .   Stress of any kind causes bodily symptoms, - contracted blood vessles etc. It may well be that part of what this mental state consists in also includes certain subliminal physiological changes which result in such things as pallor or posture typical of that kind of stress.

6.   Wittgenstein (Anscombe Trans.) 1981, §146 - §193.

7.   ibid. §143 - §199.

8.   ibid. §151.

9.   ibid. §152.
10.   ibid. §151.
11.   ibid. §181 - §191.
12.   ibid. §183.
13.   ibid. §193 - §194.
14.   In this sense, speaking or interacting socially is a creative activity and an opportunity to influence the understanding of the rules being deployed of the people to whom we speak or with whom we interact. This would seem to be part of what setting an example' amounts to.
15.   Dennett 1987.
16.   Wittgenstein (Paul & Anscombe Trans.) 1974, §417 - §420.
17.   ibid. §417.
18.   Dennett 1979, p.122.

4 An analysis of the conceptual connections of some common concepts to the human body form

So far in this essay I have concentrated on describing the limitations of the computer metaphor as elaborated by five authors. In this chapter I want to set out some fundamental conceptual limitations to the computer metaphor by showing that many of our common concepts are conceptually connected to the human form.

In the six examples which follow I want to draw out three things. First the very extensive ramifications of the conceptual connections to our concepts of having certain skills and attributes. Second, the conceptual connections between the concept of having certain skills and attributes and having certain bodily features. Third the problem this poses for any project to build an artificial person. This problem is, in a nutshell, that it would seem incoherent to ascribe many common human skills and attributes to machines as we do to people unless the machines possessed a very large further array of skills and attributes, some of which are human bodily attributes.

One

Understanding the word 'table' as people do is conceptually connected to understanding the word 'chair', to understanding simple sentences and stories containing the word table', to performing simple actions involving tables (such as putting objects on tables when asked to do so), to being able to identify tables, to knowing what kind of things tables are used for, and so on. For example, if someone understands the word 'table' then we would expect them to know what a chair is; and if we were to answer their question 'Where are the keys?' by saying They are on the 'table'. we do not expect the reply 'What is a table?'. If someone understands the word 'table' and we ask them to put a plate on the table, then, under normal circumstances we expect

77

them to be able to do so. If someone understands the word 'table' we expect them to be able to locate a table in a furniture shop (or at least not fail to do so because they can't identify tables), and if someone understands the word 'table' we expect them to be able to take part in those common activities which involve using a table (such as using it for a meal), without being given instructions as to how a table is used.

Each of these connected concepts will have its own background of conceptual connections which we would expect to hold if the first connection held in some particular case. For example if someone can put things on a table then (quadriplegics with mechanical arms apart), it is necessary for them to have the kind of body which can lift and move things. That is to say have something like an arm. Again, if someone can take part in normal activities in which tables are used (such as having a meal), we might expect them to be so constructed as to be able to sit down.

The absence in a person of any one (or even some), of these conceptually connected abilities, concepts, and further understandings will not necessarily lead us to say that the person lacks an understanding of the word 'table'. It is possible to construct cases, such as societies that do not have chairs but do have tables, and of people who have never had a meal off a table who understand the word 'table' and so on, in which any one of the conceptually connected abilities or concepts is missing but in which we would want to say that the person understands the word 'table'. It is also possible to construct cases where any one of the things I have mentioned is crucial to whether we would be prepared to say that someone understands the word 'table'. The point here is not that the possession of any particular concept or ability is *crucial* to the ascription of understanding of 'table' in all cases, rather the point is that there are certain kinds of things that we *expect* in all cases of understanding 'table' and that we can recognize as those kinds of things. It is when we have reason to doubt that someone has most of the abilities and concepts of this kind which are conceptually connected to understanding the word 'table' that we will begin to doubt that they understand the word 'table'.

The possession of each of the concepts and abilities to which I have suggested the word 'table' is conceptually connected is itself connected to other abilities and concepts.

For example, understanding the word 'chair' is conceptually connected to using chairs to sit on, understanding what a table is normally used for is conceptually connected to having uses for a table, understanding talk about tables is conceptually connected to having basic linguistic abilities, the ability to identify tables is conceptually connected to having that kind of body which can perceive in such a way that it can identify tables (in practice this means seeing), and the ability to put things on tables is conceptually connected to having a body with suitable appendages or manipulators.

The things to which the ability to understand the word 'table' is connected seem to extend, even with these few examples, to include having a body that can sit on chairs, that can see, appendages that can carry things, having uses for tables and having basic linguistic abilities. Further, having an 'appendage that can carry things' involves having the capacity to attend to or to have intentions concerning whatever the appendage is used for, - this is part of what we mean by 'using something for'. Using 'something for something' in this context involves having purposes, needs and desires with respect to tables. In order for us to be able to ascribe these to a machine in the same way as we can to persons the thing must have a sufficient richness of life for the ascription of purposes or needs or desires to make sense.

This background of things in virtue of which we would be prepared to ascribe understanding of the word 'table' appears to ramify so widely as to amount to what we might call a rudimentary kind of a life. By this I mean a sufficient richness of possibilities of action to be life-like. (I want to draw a contrast here between having life, which would apply to trees, and having *a* life, which involves having a rich capacity to act and thus does not apply to trees.) It is this richness of capacity to act in the right kind of way that we will need to see, or at least believe is present, before we can ascribe understanding of the word 'table' to something.

If a machine is to understand the word 'table' as we do then it must, for conceptual reasons, have a wide range of relevantly similar attributes to humans. One might say that tables must be able to play a similar role in the machine's life to the role they play in ours.

This indicates that for anything which is to understand one simple word, such as 'table', in the same sense as we might say that a person understands 'table', precise details of bodily structure are crucial. If the body of any purported person is not appropriate then, for conceptual reasons, we will be unwilling to say that it understands the word 'table' as normal persons do.

The manner in which the conceptual connections to 'table' ramify to all manner of other human abilities and attributes is typical of words in common use. This ramification of concepts through a language makes language like a web or a finely patterned cloth of varying texture. All parts are eventually connected to all others. We have seen that in order to be able to ascribe understanding of the word 'table' to something we would normally expect to be able to ascribe purposes, needs, or desires to it also. These in turn will have conceptual connections to other concepts, abilities, knowledge, and attributes. Taken together these further qualities when used in the sense that we normally use them of persons, will require the machine to which we would ascribe an understanding of the word 'table' to have a richness of possibilities of life approaching that of common mammals. (We wouldn't ascribe purposes, needs, and desires, in this sense, to an oyster, and would surely have doubts about a crab or a lizard.)

Similar analyses may be performed with almost any common noun or verb. Such analyses will reveal further abilities, attributes, and knowledge which a machine must have if we are to ascribe a grasp of words to it in the same sense as we ascribe them to a person. It therefore makes no sense to suppose that one might build such a machine by giving it 'one ability at a time', rather it seems that a grasp of language must be given to a machine as a single block. It is easy to convince oneself (and I shall demonstrate this in subsequent examples), that part of what I have called 'the background' to a word, the abilities, attributes, circumstances, and knowledge that are conceptually connected to a word, includes abilities to see, speak, hear, and feel by touch, all in a manner that is relevantly similar to the way humans can be said to see, speak, hear, and feel by touch.

This shows that any project to build a person which analyses the project in terms of sub-problems of building parts of a person is in error. The idea that we might build a 'vision unit', a 'speech unit', a 'touch device', and so on, and then wire them all together through a centralised co-ordinator can be seen to be clearly mistaken. Analysis of conceptual connections will show that our concept of these units (e.g. seeing a rabbit, hearing a violin), will often ramify to abilities involving other units. Thus, for example, we can expect to be able to show that in order to be able to say of something that it can see in the same sense that a person might see requires, amongst other things, that it be able to hear and feel also. Most writers who are sympathetic to the idea that a person might be built think of the project in terms of such units. For example D.C. Dennett takes this view in his paper *Towards a cognitive theory of consciousness*.[1] (I discuss this briefly in endnote 48 to chapter 2, page 46 above.) John Pollock's account of functionalism[2] commits him (as most other accounts of functionalism commit their authors), to thinking of the psyche as consisting of structures $S_1, S_2, S_3,...,S_n$, each with a specific function all of which are governed by the functional theory $T(S_1, S_2, S_3,...,S_n)$. Thus the holistic character of conceptual connections shows that the conceptual foundations of functionalism are misconceived. The discrete structural units, S_1, S_2, S_3,...,S_n, which are supposed to conform to the functional theory $T(X_1, X_2,...,X_i,...,X_n)$ where X_i is a free variable, cannot exist in human (and thus paradigmatic), persons.

This need not, of itself, prove fatal to any project to build an artificial person conceived of in this manner. It might, for example, be argued that although vision units, touch units, and such like do not really see and feel, the activity of building them allows us to achieve successive aproximations to units which, when suitably connected, would indeed see, feel, and so on.

This amounts to an empirical claim which stands in need of justification. In this context it is worth noting that when, in Mary Shelly's novel, Dr. Frankenstein connected various bits of bodies together he still had to do something further to bring the monster to life. He required 'natural electricity'. I suspect that the author needed this device to prevent the common sense of the reader declaring the plot ridiculous. Yet the situation of the monster is almost exactly analogous to the situation with the various vision units, speech units, and so on which when connected together are supposed to be a person. The philosophical point underlying this (which might appeal to A.I. enthusiasts), would be the claim that even if a human-like body is conceptually necessary for something to be a person, having the right internal structure would cause it to behave like a person. Thus the claim of strong A.I. would become that what A.I. researchers are discovering is what the appropriate internal structure for a person is like. This (the claim might go), is a step towards person-building.

I will pick up this point in the next chapter.

The next five examples will serve to show more clearly how the ramification of the conceptual connections to common words and concepts serve to bind diverse attributes of persons together in such a fashion that to ascribe one to something involves a conceptual commitment to ascribing others also.

The ability to count seems to be one of the most mechanical of abilities and one might therefore expect it to be easy to build it into machines in such a way that they have the ability in just the same way as we do. Reflection however, shows that this is not so. Just as the understanding of 'table' goes, for conceptual reasons, with a certain background so does the ability to count. Counting is an ability that requires a certain kind of background for these to be recognisable as manifestations of counting.

When the ability to count is ascribed to a machine what is meant is usually something quite different to what we mean when we ascribe it to a person. When we ascribe the ability to count to a person we expect very much more of them than the capacity to print 'the ascending sequence of positive integers starting with 1'.

For example, the ability to count is conceptually connected to being able to distinguish a group of three apples from amongst several other groups of four apples, to being able to speak the names of the integral numbers in ascending order starting at one, to the ability to point at things as one counts them, and to a certain kind of autonomy. (By this I mean that a person who can count can do so in any reasonable location, not just in one room.)

To see this, suppose a child could recite the sequence of positive integers in ascending order at great length, but could never distinguish between (by picking out) groups of three objects from groups of four. Thus even when it had recited the relevant positive integers in rhythm to putting the objects (let us say sweets) in a bag just as if it were counting them, it could not go on to distinguish the group of four similar objects (perhaps sweets or apples) from the group of three. It is unclear to me just what we would say here, probably we would ask an expert, but we would be unlikely to say that the child could count, for it could not *do* those things we mean by counting. That is to say that the ability to distinguish between groups of three apples and groups of four apples on a table is part of what we ascribe when we ascribe the ability to count. This forms part of the background which is required to ascribe coherently the ability to count. Similarly, if a child often pointed to the wrong things as it counted (some lemons on a table, for example, touching each one in turn, but doing this as it was counting some oranges and suppose that it then pointed to the lemons when it announced correctly how many oranges there were, and suppose that it did this consistently), we would doubt its ability to count. The point here is that the ability to point to the counted object as one counts forms part of the background we expect when we ascribe the ability to count. Again, if the child appeared able to exhibit the ability to count but only in one particular room at one particular desk and displayed no sign of such an ability in any other place, even when tested for it, then we would be very puzzled but would surely not say that the child could count. Our concept of what it is to be able to count leads us to expect that someone who can count can do so in any reasonably circumstances. Nor would we usually ascribe the ability to count to someone who could not recite the ascending sequence of positive integers. The ability to recite this sequence is also something we expect of people who can count.

These examples of abilities, attributes, and activities to which the ability to count is conceptually connected form part of a background which we expect when we ascribe the ability to count to someone (such as a child). In any particular case any of these may be crucial to whether we are prepared to ascribe the ability to a person; which, if any, will be crucial will depend on the particular case. The relevance of such abilities and attributes is that they form part of the background which is a constituent of what we mean by 'the ability to count'. If we are sure that all the activities and abilities of this background are missing then, no matter what the machine in question may be doing with numerals, we cannot truthfully ascribe to it the ability to count as we do. Thus if we are to ascribe the ability to count to a machine we will need to have reasonable grounds to believe (even if it is only from past experience), that this background is present.

Each of these examples of an ability, attribute, or activity to which the ability to count is conceptually connected is itself conceptually connected to other abilities, attributes, and so on.

For example, the ability to pick out a group of three apples from amongst several other groups of four apples is conceptually connected to the ability to see, to recognise common objects, to the ability to recognize when distinct objects are the same in some way, and to having an interest in counting apples. The ability to speak the names of the integral numbers in ascending order is conceptually connected to having a basic vocabulary, to being able to form sentences correctly, and to having basic language skills. The ability to count things by pointing at them is conceptually connected to having a bodily structure which makes it possible to point and to and also to having the right kind of co-ordination between the eye and the appendage used for pointing. By this I mean that the thing must have the necessary co-ordination to be able to point to a particular thing that it sees. Further,

83

in order for something to have an interest in counting apples it must have the kind of life in which it makes sense to ascribe interests to it. This ramifies very widely, for to be able to ascribe an interest to something we need to see a sufficient richness of activities and possibilities of action for it to make sense to talk in this way.

If something did indeed have such a richness of activities and possibilities and acted in a way that would lead us naturally to ascribe interests to it then (on account of the background presupposed by the possibility of ascription of interests), we would very probably feel inclined to ascribe 'a life' to it. By this I mean more than simply saying that it is alive, (as we say of trees). By 'a life' I mean all those attributes and qualities that make sense of talk about 'my life' in contrast to 'his life'. That is to say such things as a past which may be talked of in terms of 'when he was doing X' (where X is some activity), or 'when he was at Y' (where Y is a location), a future which may be thought of in terms of possibilities of action or ways of living, a way of living which consists of dispositions to action which are typical or distinctive of him, and so on. In this way our concept of the ability to count is conceptually connected to much of our ordinary activity of life.

It is possible to find examples such that we would be prepared to ascribe the ability to count to a person who lacked any one of these abilities (except perhaps that of having interests), however it is not the presence of particular attributes that is crucial to the ascription but the presence of a background of certain kinds of attributes, abilities, and so on. Thus, that a dumb person can count does not undermine this analysis of the ability to count. The dumb person still has a sufficient background of abilities for talk of them counting to make sense. Equally the fact that we talk of a person counting under his breath does not undermine this analysis. When we talk thus we do not doubt that the person possesses all the necessary background abilities, it is simply that he is not manifesting them. These people are able to count and, if we are in doubt, we may test them for the conceptually connected abilities that make up the background.

In this way the ability to count ramifies in its conceptual connections to the abilities to talk, to point, to recognize common objects, to recognise 'sameness' between objects, to arm-eye (or 'pointing appendage'-eye), co-ordination, to having an interest in counting things, and to a certain kind of autonomy. From this it seems that part of the background that goes with the ability to count as we do is a certain body form: Something that counts as we do must have something that serves the purpose of eyes, something that serves as an appendage for pointing, and a degree of co-ordination between them. For each of these attributes there will in turn be a further background of attributes that we will expect for their ascription, and so on. These ramifications of what goes to make up the background that we require for the ascription of the ability to count can reach out to very diverse things. It seems clear that if these connections were teased out further the expected background could be seen to be a kind of a life. That is to say that the activities would be sufficiently similar to our activities of life for them to be recognizable as the activities of a life.

Now if the ability to count as we do is to be ascribed to a machine that has been built, it will need to exhibit a background of activities, abilities, and attributes that is relevantly similar to the one which we have. For any project to build a person by simulation[3] this example makes explicit the deep problems I noted above (pages 78-80). First, there appears to be a problem of almost unlimited ramification of conceptual connections to basic abilities. This makes the complexity of what is to be simulated huge, possibly increasing combinatorially with the number of abilities, activities, and attributes. (It is possible that it is actually infinite.) Second, there is a problem that part of what the ramified background amounts to is a requirement for a body that is substantially similar to our own. This similarity will become clear with further examples. It seems very likely that if we were to trace out all the ramifications not only of the things conceptually connected to counting but of the things conceptually connected to these and to all further such connections we would find that each chain of connections ended either in a fact of physiology, or a fact about the physical world, or a fact about our simplest dispositions to respond. From the following examples it will become clear that these conceptually necessary facts about our physiology render incoherent any attempt at simulation[3] of a person which is not also to some extent an attempt at replication[3] of a person.

Three

Next I want to examine when we would be prepared to ascribe an understanding of the concepts of 'hardness' and 'Softness' to someone or something.

The concepts of hardness' and 'softness' can easily seem to be concepts of qualities which inhere in objects themselves and are largely independent of circumstances or background. The hardness of a stone has a kind of irreducible quality to it. The softness of fur seems inherent in its being fur. To some extent this is true. Part of our concept of 'hardness' is the property of being unyielding to pressure and difficult to deform, and part of our concept of 'softness' is the property of yielding to pressure and being easy to deform. I shall argue that these properties can only be what they are in the context of a background of human abilities, attributes, circumstances, knowledge and similar things and that the concepts of 'hardness' and 'softness', like all other concepts, are conceptually connected to other abilities, attributes, knowledge, concepts, and other things, many of which we will expect to be present in a person who has grasped these concepts.

If someone has grasped the concept of 'hardness' then we would expect them to behave differently towards hard things than they would towards soft things. For example, if a human were to sit down on a concrete surface in the fashion in which they would normally sit down on a sofa they would certainly bruise themselves. If someone is handling a sharp steel knife they usually take some care with it, for example avoiding rubbing the sharp edge of it across their hands by mistake.

Similarly, if someone has grasped the concept of 'softness' we will expect them to behave differently towards soft objects compared to the way they behave towards hard objects. Thus a rubber knife will not normally be handled with the same care as would a steel knife, and if all other circumstances are the same a person sitting in a normal armchair will be more relaxed than someone sitting in a similar chair made of concrete. Usually soft things are unlikely to cut or bruise us.

If someone did not vary their behaviour as I have described it as a consequence of knowing that objects are hard or soft then we would probably think them mad. If this person (incredibly) for some reason simply did not understand that he could be bruised and cut by some objects but not by others, then he would be lacking a crucial part of the background to the concepts of 'hardness' and 'softness'. 'hardness' and 'softness' are internally related to knowing that some things, handled or treated in a particular way, are likely to cut and bruise, whereas others are not. We take the particular kind of care concerning what we do with hard objects because we are soft and fleshy creatures and can therefore easily be hurt (which is something we are disposed to avoid). We are able to find some soft things ease inducing and relaxing also in virtue of being soft and fleshy creatures. By way of an imaginary contrast, we cannot know what kind of things an 'iron man' (a science fiction artificial person with an iron body) would find relaxing, but there is no reason to suppose that they would be the same things as we find relaxing.

If we were not soft and fleshy, or if cutting and bruising ourselves was always quite irrelevant to how we behaved (perhaps in such a world all wounds heal instantly), then a part of what we mean by 'hard object' would have disappeared. Our concept of 'hardness' would have changed. Those things which we regard as hard are things which affect us or have the potential to affect us in certain ways. We are so affected by 'hard objects' because our bodies have certain physical properties. For example, our flesh deforms easily if touched gently when we are relaxed, yet is much more resilient when deformed a little bit more by stretching. Our skin is acutely sensitive to a gentle touch, but not sensitive in proportion to pressure. Thus a blow does not feel in proportion to the extent to which its force exceeds the force of a caress. All these physiological facts are relevant to the kinds of thing we are able, unable, willing and unwilling to do with hard objects. Our concept of 'hardness' reflects the limitations to our actions and the possibilities of action open to us that we have in virtue of our bodies having some of the properties that they do. If our bodies were substantially different (suppose that they were made of steel), then we could not make sense of our current concepts of 'hardness' and 'softness' for we would not be able to use these words as we now do. They could not find application in the lives of the people of such a society as they do in our lives.

For example, if we can imagine a person made of steel, or who is effectively invulnerable, then we do not imagine them cutting themselves on a sharp kitchen knife. An invulnerable person would not show the same caution as we do in his actions when using knives and chisels. We could see that sharpness or hardness was different for them. It would not matter to them in the same way as it does to us. We could see that hard things and sharp things have different potentials for such persons than they do for us. Such persons could not have the concepts of 'hardness' and 'softness' for they behave in a manner that is inconsistent with having them. If they did exhibit the same caution in handling a sharp knife as we exhibit yet we knew them to be invulnerable then we would expect a further explanation: Fear of cutting oneself when one is uncuttable, or fear of grazing oneself when one is ungrazeable are, by themselves, incomprehensible. Such behaviour would require further explanation for it to be comprehensible (perhaps they are mad). If we observed them reacting to hard and soft objects just as we do we would probably understand their actions as having a deeper motive. We would understand them as having a reason for acting in this way. What I take this example to show is that if something has a body that is different to ours in certain respects then their life will be very different and this will result in their concepts being very different.

This difference between their world and ours would show in the simplest of actions. They would handle sharp instruments differently, they would be less careful with their limbs (shutting their fingers in the door would be a trivial matter for them), they would be prone to take risks in driving that we would not (invulnerability makes car crashes more bearable), and so on. From the simplest precautions to their social organisation (for example the role that fighting plays in the lives of their children), they would be noticeably different from us. Thus it seems inconceivable that we would ascribe understanding of the concepts of 'hardness' and 'softness' to someone who was invulnerable in the same way as we ascribe them to human persons.

What I take this to show is that for anything which is to grasp our concepts of 'hardness' and 'softness' bodily structure is crucial. If something does not have a bodily structure that is relevantly similar to ours then it will not be able to grasp our concepts of 'hardness' and 'softness'.

The importance of this for person building will depend on how far this lacuna would affect the behaviour of a hypothetical artificial person which had a significantly different bodily structure to our one. If such a thing's behaviour is sufficiently alien to us then the word person' will not get application to it. My next example shows that many of the capacities that we tend to think of as distinctive of persons would only get application to something that had a body that was similar to a human body in many detailed respects.

Four

Suppose we describe a particular bodily movement as a caress, then, if the movement is indeed a caress we will expect a large number of other things to be true about the thing which is caressing. Part of this will be that it has the right kind of structure. It is not sufficient that the body be made of some substance which is soft and deforms a bit as ours does and that happens to be pressure sensitive. Much more is required: If the movement is indeed a caress then we would expect that it will have many further dispositions and abilities and that many further hypotheticals about its life and the role that a caress might play in its life, would be true.

For example, if something is capable of giving a caress then, under normal circumstances, we will expect that amongst other things it will be able to express affection, to be intimate, to exhibit emotional warmth, to care for others, to feel concern for others, to love, to trust as normal people do, and many other similar things. The capacity to caress, being commonly an expression of any of these attitudes, is conceptually connected to all of them. That is to say that if we were to come across something which lacked a capacity for sufficient of these kinds of attitudes we would be unwilling to describe any behaviour it might exhibit as a caress in the same sense as we normally use that word.

If we are to say something is able to express affection then it must make sense to ascribe affection to it. The concept of affection can only find application to something if it has the right kind of life. That is to say that if we can make sense of it having a rich repertoire of possible emotions such as being angry, or lonely, or resentful, or reassured, or comforted, or hurt, or frightened, and so on. If something never showed any sign of any of these emotions, but occasionally behaved affectionately, then I think we would doubt that its 'affection' was what we normally call affection. In this sense it would not be real affection. This is not to say that any one of these emotions is crucial as a background to the ascription of affection, but it is to say that in order for it to make sense to ascribe affection to something it must live in circumstances which yield the possibilities of action and a social organisation which are sufficiently complex for such an ascription to make sense. This is part of what we mean when we say of something that it has a life. (Discussed above pages 79 and 84.)

Exactly the same kind of considerations apply to the other attributes and abilities that I have listed above as forming a part of the background that we expect to go with a capacity to caress. Thus if something is able to be intimate we would expect it to be able to be trusting, to be vulnerable, to be reassured, to be angry, to be relaxed, to be resentful, to be sensitive, to be able to cry, to be loving, and so on. None of these are crucial to a capacity for intimacy but if sufficient of them were missing from the repertoire of behaviour of something then we would doubt that anything we saw it do could be an expression of intimacy, for the grounds for the application of the word would have been removed.

An almost identical argument will run for the ability to exhibit emotional warmth, to care for others, to feel concern for others, to love, and to trust in a normal fashion. For all these it only makes sense to ascribe them to something if that something has a rich repertoire of further capacities to feel and to exhibit emotions. These concepts are such that they only find a comprehensible application (when used in a common or normal sense) to something that has adequate possibilities of action and richness of life.

Such a rich background of emotions and feelings itself can only be ascribed against a further background of capacities to act in ways that we would understand as appropriate to expressing emotions. Thus such concepts as those of being lonely (that is to say what lonely people do, rather than our concept of loneliness), being angry, being resentful, being reassured, being comforted, behaving in a hurt fashion, being vulnerable, being sensitive, crying, being loving, being anxious, reacting to a loving touch by all our awareness becoming focused in the touch, feeling tension or relaxation in someone's skin texture or tone, kissing, and many other similar things all are conceptually connected to being able to touch appropriately in appropriate circumstances as humans touch in those circumstances.

Touching, in this context, means far more than contiguous contact, it means all those ways of acting and reacting towards another person which involve the expression of feeling through bodily contact. For this kind of touching to be possible it is necessary that the body be like the human body in considerable detail. The kinds of feelings and emotions that I have listed which can find expression through touch are conceptually connected to, amongst other things, the following physiological details: Having arms and legs, having hands which can bend in such a fashion as to be able to follow the contours of a body, having a body that varies in sensitivity from place to place, having a body that varies in sensitivity with mood, having flesh (muscles) that can be taut or relaxed, having flesh that reacts to stress, to tension, to resistance, and to steeling oneself for a blow and such like things by becoming hard (the muscles 'tensing up'), having a bodily sense that can be aware of limb position or muscle state without visual observation, having a body such that tension can lead to pains in the neck or a racing heart, having a body that is capable of shaking with fear and of sweating with anxiety and so on.

Once again, my argument is not that any one of these is crucial to the possibility of coherent ascription of those emotions and feelings which can be expressed through bodily touch, but that if sufficient of such bodily attributes, capacities and powers are missing from something then we will have doubts about ascribing or even find it impossible to ascribe those emotions and feelings to it. These kinds of emotions and feelings that are expressible through bodily touch are conceptually connected to the details of bodily structure that I have listed.

It seems that all parts or aspects of the human body that can be perceived or which play a role in the nature of what a person perceives can, in virtue of being so perceptible, form a part of a background to a feeling or emotion which can be expressed through touch. If this is correct then the background of bodily structure, that is conceptually connected to the emotions and feelings that can be expressed through touch include all anatomical details which are common to most human bodies and which can reliably influence what and how we feel. This includes such diverse things as how the hand is constructed (that a handshake may be limp or firm), skin that can be warm or clammy, the capacity to grow calluses and the capacity to have stomach aches from overeating.

The implications of this for any project to build a person are very great. If something is so different from us that it has no room for many of our most intimate activities then it is unlikely that we would be willing to call it a person. If something had such a bodily structure that we were unable to ascribe to it any of the feelings and emotions that can be expressed through touch, then it would surely seem 'mechanical' in the sense of being unlike a person. Something of this kind, to which we could not ascribe such feelings and emotions would also be unable to take part in the normal social activities that we expect of persons. They would suffer from the ultimate social ostracism: Lacking all such emotions and feelings (for the very concepts will not admit of their ascription to such things) they would be blind to the 'human' world of persons and incapable of being invited or drawn into it. They could not be thought of as persons.

Thus, for something to be able to caress, to be able to express affection, to be intimate, to exhibit emotional warmth, to care for others, to feel concern for others, to love, to trust as normal people do, to be comforted, to be hurt, to be happy, to cry, or to be capable of any other emotion or feeling which can be expressed through touch, it must, for conceptual reasons, have a bodily anatomy that is the same as a human body in any respect which, in a human, might regularly influence how and what we feel by touch. In the absence of all these qualities and capacities a thing could not be thought of as a person. Thus, in order for something to be a person it is crucial that, in all sensually perceptible details, it have a body that is sufficiently like a human body for it to make sense to ascribe to it the emotions and feelings which can be expressed through touch and touching.

For any project to build a person this poses difficult constraints. It would not be sufficient for an artificial person to have a body vaguely similar to that of a human person. Such a thing would not be in a position analogous to a severely handicapped and deformed human. A handicapped human has a distinctively human history, mother and father, body, and most human anatomical structures. Such a person is, in most respects, just like us. An alleged artificial person does not have a human history or parents. That is one reason why its moral status is in doubt. For these reasons an alleged artificial person must be clearly a fully fledged person, and obviously so. From the preceding discussion of touching, we can see that this requires it to have the same kinds of concern and interest in how it touches and is touched as humans do. This means, in all sensually perceptible respects, having a body which is very similar to a human body. From this discussion it is clear that Pollock's comment about persons and can openers (discussed above page 42), is mistaken.

Five

Next I want to consider when we are prepared to say that someone understands the word 'Spring' as we do, and what must, for conceptual reasons, be true of him in order that he may understand the word 'Spring' as we do. Those things that will make it true that someone understands the word 'Spring' will be the mass of conceptual connections to the word 'Spring' that we will expect a native English speaker to have and to be able to display in their speech and actions. In order that someone may be able to understand the word 'Spring' it must be possible for them to display those conceptual connections to a background of knowledge, understanding, expectations and concepts to which the word 'Spring' is conceptually connected. I shall show that it can only make sense to ascribe these conceptual connections to someone if they have the appropriate capacities to act and react to 'Spring-like' changes in the environment.

If someone understands the word 'Spring' then our concept is such that we will expect them to know what an april shower is, and to be aware that Spring in England is accompanied by changes in the visual texture of the landscape as new growth sets into plants, we will expect them to expect that in Spring in England the Sun and air begin to feel more substantial in their warmth, and we will expect them to understand about the changes in people's behaviour that come about on account of the lengthening of daylight in the evenings and many other things conceptually connected to 'Spring'.

92

To see these particular connections we need only consider what we would say if someone 'got them wrong'. Ignorance of april showers would not, by itself, usually, indicate a failure to understand the word 'Spring'. Suppose, however, that in a conversation (far from Britain) it transpired that the person we were talking to thought that rainfall in Britain followed the monsoon pattern. We would surely doubt that he understood the english word 'Spring'. Similarly, if someone should demonstrate an ignorance concerning the onset of new growth that comes with Spring in Britain we would doubt that he understood the word 'Spring'. The same may be said for the expectation of increasing warmth that is a feature of our concept of 'Spring'. One cannot coherently think of Spring in terms of persisting cold and frost (in terms that are 'wintery'). Again, if someone were to demonstrate an ignorance of the way Spring affects people's behaviour (say a child drawing a picture of Spring in which people's attire, demeanour, and activities were those of Winter), we would doubt that he understood the word 'Spring'.

If someone knows what an april shower is then for conceptual reasons we will expect them to be able to understand the role that april showers play in our lives. This would consist in demonstrating similar conceptual connections to april showers to those that we have, that is to say having the appropriate background against which it makes sense to say that they know what an april shower might be. Thus if someone understands what an april shower is we would expect them to understand what waterproof clothing is and how and why it is used. (This would show in their conversation.) We might expect them to show knowledge of and understanding of the motivation to the practice of running from shop door to shop door in order to avoid getting wet (that is to say what it is like to get wet in the rain and why we try to avoid it). We would expect them to be able to talk about and make sense of talk about the feel of rain on the cheek and the differences between this in Spring and in Winter.

This knowledge and these understandings and ideas are themselves each conceptually connected to a further background which we must believe is present in someone or something for it to be possible coherently to ascribe them to some person or thing. For example, there are abilities, concepts, and knowledge of facts that we expect someone to have who understands what waterproof clothing is and how to put it on: We would not readily say that someone knew what waterproof clothing is and how and why it is used if they had no idea how to put it on. (This is not the same as having difficulty putting on a particular article of clothing.) If we say someone is able to put on waterproof clothing then we expect them, amongst other things, to have the kind of body and bodily powers (for example, be able to lift things, put them over, round, or on themselves, be self-mobile, and so on), which are necessary for putting on waterproof clothing. Thus by a chain of connections the ability to understand the word 'Spring' is conceptually connected to having the kind of body which has the requisite form and powers for putting on waterproof clothing.

If we are to say of someone that they show knowledge of and understanding of the motivation to the practice of running from shop door to shop door in order to avoid getting wet then our concept is such that we will expect them to know what a shop and a shop door are, what it is to get wet, and why people generally want to avoid it. If someone knows what a shop is then, for conceptual reasons, we will expect them to be able to go into one and be able to buy things, to point them out, and so on. (Under normal circumstances complete inability to do these kinds of thing would suggest that someone did not know what a shop is.)

If someone knows what it is like to get wet and why people generally want to avoid it then this will show in their talk, actions, and behaviour. We will be unlikely to say that someone knows what it is like to get wet if they do not react in a manner we recognise as human-like to getting wet or the prospect of getting wet. Thus our concepts lead us to expect a certain kind of behaviour from someone who knows what it is like to get wet. What this behaviour will look like can vary enormously: The reactions to being thrown in the fountain (or the threat of it) on Rag Day are quite different to those of an invitation to a swimming party. Nonetheless if on a cold and breezy day someone whose clothes were soaked did not display any signs of needing to change their clothes, dry themselves, or keep warm, then we would be at least surprised. If they showed no signs of shivering with cold we would be further surprised (and if we knew them to normal human beings perhaps somewhat alarmed for their health). If someone never showed any awareness of the differences in temperature of water that touched him then we should doubt his soundness of mind or of body. Certainly, if all these were true of a machine we would doubt that it could feel the wetness of water as we do. Thus we may say that the ability to understand the word 'Spring' is conceptually connected to having the kind of body that will react to hot and cold and which will feel comfort and discomfort according to the circumstances in which it is wet and dry as ours does.

If someone was aware that Spring in Britain is accompanied by change in the visual texture of the landscape as new growth sets into plants we would expect such a person to know what plants are, to be aware that many of them grow in a cyclical pattern through the year, to be able to see and distinguish visual textures, to be able to explain what growth (in a plant) is, and so on.

If someone does indeed know what plants are then we will expect them to be able to point to them and by touching, smelling, looking and possibly tasting them to distinguish correctly (in most cases), between what is a plant and what is not, to know in what kind of place one normally finds plants, and to know a little about what they do and don't do (e.g. get up and walk, grow, talk) and so on. We would surely (under normal circumstances), have doubts about whether a person knows what plants are if he could not reliably or usually distinguish between those things that are plants and those which are not, or if he had no idea in what kind of place one might normally expect to find plants, or if he had no conception of the kinds of things one may usually expect of plants (for example, suppose he thought plants were talkative).

The third example I gave of things we would expect (for conceptual reasons) of someone who understands the word 'Spring' was that *we* would expect *them* to expect that in Spring in England the Sun and air begin to feel more substantial in their warmth. If someone really expects this then we (for conceptual reasons) will expect that if they were in England in Spring they would display a wealth of appropriate behavioural traits in their concerns, actions, subjects of speech, tone of voice, hesitations, rhythms of speech when talking on associated subjects, reactions to others, (expressions of surprise, hope, etc.) and their dispositions to act. For example, they would notice and perhaps pass comment if the new warmth were late in coming, they would perhaps purchase new plants for their garden, would perhaps send their winter coat to be dry cleaned and use a light 'mac' as a waterproof instead, and even if they were not in England would indicate in their speech, particularly if asked, or in letters they might write that they expect that this is the kind of thing people in England would be doing at this time of year.

Now apart form very specialised or constrained circumstances I do not think that any of the manifestations of expecting something that we might expect a person who is expecting something to display, are generally crucial to the ascription of expectation. That is to say that I do not think we can say of any of the examples that I have given or of any others that might be given that in most normal circumstances if that feature is missing then we will not, for conceptual reasons, be able truthfully to say that we believe that some person expects that in Spring in England the Sun and air begin to feel more substantial in their warmth. I do, however, think that features of a person's life of the mind that I have listed are conceptually required for us to be able to ascribe such a state of expecting. It is when we see sufficient behavioural traits of this kind that we are prone to ascribe a state of expecting. These behavioural traits might be characterized by a sense of pointing forward, that is to say being appropriate to a state of affairs which has not yet come about but the person believes might quite easily come to pass soon. I want to say that a sufficiency of these kinds of behavioural traits that we could notice are a crucial part of our concept of what it is to expect something. It is as if to expect something is to undergo a change in the colour, mood, or tone of our disposition to act. It is quite consistent with this indefinite quality of our concept that the ascription of expecting something to someone is less certain and more easily thrown into doubt (and thus apparently less substantial) than most other mental predicates. Nonetheless, of all things of the kind I have listed, such as passing comment if the new warmth were late in coming, or buying new plants for the garden, or sending their winter coats to be dry-cleaned, were missing, then we would surely not be inclined to say that this person expected that in Spring in England the Sun and air begin to feel more substantial in their warmth.

The examples I have given of things that are conceptually connected to expecting that in Spring in England the Sun and air begin to feel more substantial in their warmth only make sense if ascribed to a person with a certain background of attributes. For example, in order for it to make sense to speak of someone passing comment if the warm weather is late in coming in they must be the kind of being of whom it makes sense to suppose that they have concerns about the weather, that can communicate with one another, that can share expectations, and who have a sense of time. It is not difficult to see that the conceptual connections to these ramify almost as widely as life itself: In order for it to make sense to say that someone has concerns about the weather they must at least be aware of it. In this context having concerns only makes sense if they are materially affected by the weather (since a comment in this context is more than simply uttering a proposition). Saying someone is materially affected by the weather only makes sense if the person has a body that is sensitive in some way to changes in the weather. (That someone may be able to ignore the weather is not analogous to a machine being insensitive to the weather but able to measure the temperature and moisture content of the atmosphere and similar things. The capacity to ignore the weather is something that will itself have a conceptual background and is done be choice.)

This kind of analysis of the background of ideas, activities, concepts, and experiences which are conceptually connected to the ability to understand the word 'Spring' could be repeated for almost any vocabulary that is commonly used to describe the weather and climate, scents and flavours, many aspects of music, fashion and much of the visual arts. Almost anything whose most immediate and primary impact on us we would describe as some kind of sensation could be subject to a similar analysis, for such things are almost always ones which lead us to act or behave in direct response to the way our bodies are affected by the environment.

We do not expect all persons to be affected by any one of these in a like manner or to have exactly the same conceptually connected background to any of this vocabulary, but we do expect people with a good grasp of the language to find the majority of common perceptions in these matters comprehensible. By this I mean to be able to make sense of most of what people say on these subjects. For example, we do not expect all people to understand or share all the perceptions of a perfumier, but we do expect most people to be able to understand why Lavender is said to be an invigorating scent. The basic vocabulary of these areas of discourse is founded in having a disposition to respond to stimuli in a certain way. This in turn is founded (in part) on having the kind of body that we do. These dispositions form a background which we expect of anyone who understands the vocabulary of such discourse. In order to have such a background a person needs a body with the right kinds of sensitivities.

For any project to build a person this presents further constraints on what may reasonably be expected to succeed. At the end of the previous section on touch I argued that in all sensually perceptible respects the body of an artificial person must be the same as that of a human. This analysis of 'Spring' has shown that for it to make sense to ascribe to something a grasp of the meaning of words and concepts used to describe things whose most immediate impact on us is some kind of sensation it is necessary that that thing have a body which is able to respond to stimuli and sensory change just as a human body does. For example, its reaction to hot and cold, wet and dry, its repertoire of possible reactions to scents and differences in colour, its ability to discriminate sounds, its capacity to taste and so on must be much as they are for a human. This is not to say that they must be identical with those of some particular human, there is, after all, considerable variation between people in this respect, however, its basic repertoire of reactions must be recognisably those of a person. These, as we have seen, form a crucial part of the background which is necessary if something can be said to understand the language of sensory discourse.

Six

In the preceding five examples I have taken a human skill or attribute and traced some features of the background that is required for its ascription. Our concepts of these attributes and skills require that there be a background of further attributes, skills, and concepts before they can be ascribed. Amongst these background attributes I have traced certain bodily attributes. That is to say we would not normally be prepared to ascribe the skills and attributes I set out to analyse if the subject did not have the right kind of body.

If it is possible for something to be in pain, then it will be possible to pity it. This is because the concept of pain is conceptually connected to the concept of pity. (I owe this insight to Dr. D.A. Cockburn.) To see this let us try to imagine someone that we supposed to have a clear grasp of the concept of pain yet had no notion of pity.

In saying that someone grasps the concept of pain we mean that they understand such things as the following: Why it is that someone without shoes on who has just stubbed their toe hard has tears welling up in his eyes and has just sat down precipitously and is holding his toe. Why someone whose boots give them a blister while out walking limps, and so on. We also expect that they would be able to feel for and to feel with someone in pain. For example, if someone knew, while out hill walking, that one of his party was limping badly because he had a blister that was causing him pain, but showed no signs of caring, concern, or fellow feeling for the person in pain, we would doubtless describe him as callous, or hard hearted, or brutish, or something similar. If however we were to mention this to them, and they were to show every sign of incomprehension, and if, further, they were to assert things that showed that it never occurred to them to show any sign of fellow feeling for the person with a limp (such as commiserating, or taking special account of their situation), and were to ask with genuine puzzlement why anyone should do things that show fellow feeling, then we would probably think that they had failed to understand the situation or failed to understand that the person was in pain. If it further transpired that they understood that the person limping was indeed in pain yet that they quite failed to apprehend that there was any sense in which a display of fellow feeling flowed naturally from these circumstances (this all supposes that we do not conclude that this person is simply being obdurate or playing a silly game), then we would surely be forced to conclude that there was something badly amiss with this person's grasp of the concept of pain. They would not have grasped the concept of pain. It seems to me that the idea of someone being in pain and the tendency to display fellow feeling are so closely bound together that this example, in which one is present without the other, is difficult to imagine clearly. This is a measure of how tight the conceptual connection between pain and fellow feeling is. It seems to me therefore, that in the total absence of a capacity for fellow feeling of this kind a person could not truthfully be said to have understood the concept of pain.

This kind of fellow feeling is a crucial part of the concept of pity. Pity devoid of such fellow feeling would not be pity. Any case of such 'pity-devoid-of-fellow-feeling' would be mere going through the motions of pitying. It would, if detected, appear as a charade. Thus a grasp of the concept of pity is crucial to a grasp of the concept of pain. We cannot ascribe a grasp of the concept of pain to something without also ascribing a grasp of the concept of pity for others in virtue of being in pain.

This conclusion applies to ourselves with the same force as it would to any machine that might be presented as a candidate for personhood. If we believe something to be in pain then we must be able to pity it. It is also true that if we are able to pity something because we believe it to be in pain, then we must believe it to be the kind of thing which is capable of having pains. Further, if it should turn out that we are quite unable to pity something under any circumstances, then either we can not believe that it could ever have pains in the sense that a person can have pains, or our grasp of the concept of pain is deficient. Thus a prerequisite for a thing being the kind of thing that can have pains is that the thing in question be the kind of thing that could, under suitable circumstances, be pitied by most normal language users. It makes no sense to suppose that a thing might have pains yet not be capable of being pitied, for, as we have seen above, a conceptual analysis of the concept of pain shows that anything which has grasped the concept of pain must have grasped the concept of pity also. This is part of what it is for us to have a full grasp of the concept of pain. In wittgensteinian jargon we can say that the concepts of pain and pity are internally related.

There are some things that it is obvious that we can pity, such as suffering children, and some things that it is obvious that we cannot, such as stones. There are also plenty of things about which we might have doubts whether they can ever be pitied; for example, most species of fish. One thing which we expect of all persons is that under the right circumstances they could be regarded with pity. We can therefore expect that any machine which we are to suppose might be a person will be the kind of thing which clearly could, under suitable circumstances, be pitied.

Such an observation constrains the kind of thing we may regard as a person. If I can specify the kinds of things that we will expect to be true of something that can be pitied then I will also have specified some of the kinds of things that we would expect to be true of any machine which is to be a candidate for personhood.

A paradigm case of something which we would naturally pity, it seems to me, is a child suffering from terminal cancer. Our pity is provoked by the child in its situation. Particular aspects of the case however act potently to draw forth in us feelings of pity. Examples of this are perhaps that the child (let us say a girl), is clearly in pain, that she puts on a brave face and pretends not to be in pain, that against all that we and the child know to be probable she insists on talking about the future and what she will do when she gets out of hospital, that when she lapses into thoughts about death she speaks to her teddy as if it will be 'coming with her', that she never complains when her treatment is painful, and so on. These, and many things like these, are the kinds of things we would expect would be true of a child suffering from terminal cancer. This list might be extended at great length. It seems certain that if we were to make such an extended list and were to imagine a situation in which many entries from the list were missing then, if sufficient were missing, we would find that we were imagining a case in which we were unconvinced that the child was in pain and in which we did not feel greatly moved to pity simply on account of her being in pain.

For such a repertoire of behaviour, or anything remotely like it, to be possible for something requires that it have very many facets of a human life. For example, for us to be able to say that something is in pain requires amongst other things that it have the kind of body we can understand as being sensitive, that it recoil from any source of pain, that it show a reluctance to repeatedly expose itself to the source of pain, that it tend to exhibit some kind of strategy for avoiding the source of pain, and so on. For something to be capable of showing bravery of the kind I described requires amongst other things that it be capable of different kinds of reaction towards pain of which we would judge that some are easier and some more difficult for it and of which the more difficult ones are those which involve a greater exposure to pain or inhibiting those reactions and behaviour which make other people uncomfortable and uneasy (thus in some sense passing the disturbing quality of the pain onto them), and which involve the kind of intensity and single-mindedness of purpose which we associate with gritting one's teeth.

For it to make sense to ascribe qualities such as single-mindedness or gritting of teeth requires that it make sense to talk about the thing being happy and unhappy, being at ease and stressed, and such like. In turn part of what is required for ascriptions such as these are a body which can display its states in its surface qualities (such as muscle tone), which can display an ease of movement such as is characteristic of ease and happiness and which can display the rigidity and jerky qualities which are characteristic of stress and unhappiness.

Another kind of thing which is required for ascriptions of bravery of this kind to make sense is that the display of bravery be made in a society which has space for value judgements about bravery and cowardice and which has the necessary practices for such distinctions to make sense. By this I mean such things as preferring the expression of pleasant feelings to unpleasant feelings, of expressing distress, of helping others who are in distress (or at least members of certain groups when they are in distress), of caring about others, and so forth. In the absence of things of this kind distinctions between bravery and cowardice would not make sense.

Ascriptions of bravery and cowardice in turn require that a thing be part of a society with social practices, in which the members can communicate their states of happiness or ease or stress or pain and such like to one another. These kinds of qualities require for their ascription, amongst other things, that the thing have an area of its body and an organ (like the eye in the face) which is particularly expressive of feeling of emotional state. To be able to talk to others about the future or to a stuffed toy about 'going somewhere after death' requires amongst many other things, a rich language with a tense structure and a grasp of abstract concepts. To be able to pretend requires an ability to know what is expected of you and what kind of behaviour will elicit particular kinds of reaction and many other things. In consequence, we may say that in a paradigm case where we would feel pity the kinds of things that we expect to hold true include such things as a body which can display its states in its surface qualities, can move lightly and easily or rigidly and jerkily, which is part of a society in which there are normal practices of helping the distressed and of caring about others, in which communication of feeling is possible, which has a language which supports a tense structure and abstract concepts, and of which the members have something like, in relevant respects, a face with eyes.

Another, less paradigmatic, case of something we would pity would be a dog which had been hit by a car and which was lying at the side of the road with a broken leg. The reason why we would pity it would be that it was suffering and that we felt for its suffering. The kinds of thing that we would expect to be true in such a case and which would be likely to move us to pity would include such things as, that it was whimpering, that it was shivering, that its eyes were imploring help, that it held out its leg, that it yelped when it we touched its leg, that it held itself stiff when we lifted it, and so on. These are the kinds of thing we would expect to be true of a suffering animal like a dog which was in great pain and in such circumstances. If sufficient things of this kind were not true then we would be prone to doubt that the dog was in pain and would not be inclined to pity it.

In order for it to be possible for these kinds of thing to be true of something other things must also be true: For example, for something to be able to whimper it must not only be able to make sounds but be the kind of thing which we would expect to have a repertoire of sounds some of which are forceful and life asserting (such as barking), and some of which are gentle and comfort seeking (such as whimpering). For this to be possible it must be the kind of thing which has a sufficiently rich repertoire of behaviours for it to make sense for us to associate one set of sounds with forceful, outgoing, life asserting behaviour, and another with more gentle, comfort, welcome, social contact, and attention seeking behaviours. In turn, for these to be possible, requires a huge variety of kinds of life to be possible: For example, for behaviour to be forceful, outgoing, and life asserting, requires, amongst other things, that the thing be clearly alive, that it be capable of things like running, jumping, turning, chasing, being chased, playing, and so on. It would be very difficult to say that something which was quite incapable of all these things was behaving in a life asserting way and to mean this literally. (Sloths are simply not life asserting animals, - and they can turn.) To be able to run requires legs. (In the case of fish, it seems to me that while they can appear life-asserting in a Walt Disney cartoon, in the rivers of Britain they behave as they do as part of a more or less mechanical response to the environment. Perhaps they are a borderline case.) To chase and be chased requires the ability to follow something, to display intent, to display fear and pleasure, and to show in its motion and bodily state that it has been pushed in its exertions to the extremities of its bodily capacity. In practice this means such things as being able to sweat, to look dishevelled, and to move the limbs when running hard in such a fashion that, if they were to move any more vigorously in the same fashion they would have performed the impossible. In this I have in mind the appearance that an animal has when running as fast as possible. It seems that the animal could not possibly take larger steps and our sense of rhythm tells us that for an animal of that size and shape it is not possible to take the steps faster and still look like an animal. If it did it would look, as we would say, 'unnatural'. (It is noteworthy in this context that rotating wheels quite fail to convey any sense of being at their limit, however fast they may turn.)

To be able to display fear and pleasure, and the extremity of exertion involved in chasing and being chased requires a face which can be expressive. For it to make sense to speak of something as playing or being playful requires, amongst other things, that it be part of a society, that it has grown up in a society, and that the behaviour of the young in that society can be seen as copying the behaviour of the adults in an apparently purposeless yet deliberate and spontaneous way. It would be difficult to describe something as playing if it did not have a young phase of life and an adult phase in either of which it typically exhibited contrasting behaviour to the behaviour it typically exhibited in the other.

Thus, after only a very brief examination we may say that in order for it to make sense to ascribe pain to and to be able to pity something as we might an injured dog we would expect it to have legs, to be able to follow something, to be able to become dishevelled, to be part of a society, to have distinct juvenile and adult phases, and such like things. We would expect these things for conceptual reasons, for if something lacked many of these things then our concepts of pity and pain would start to seem less appropriate in that case. If something lacked sufficient of these kinds of things then we would no longer ascribe pain to it or pity it. Our concepts of pain and pity require things of these kinds for their literal application: The story of the electric beetle by Terrel Miender[4] only serves to illustrate how easily we could be temporarily fooled into pitying something by only a few of the right kind of things being present in appropriate circumstances.

What I have shown in this section on pain and pity is that pain and pity are internally related and require, for conceptual reasons, certain kinds of things to be true of anything to which we may apply them if they are to get application in their normal paradigmatic sense. These things include a body which displays its states in its surface qualities, which can move lightly and easily or rigidly and jerkily, that has legs, is able to sweat and to become dishevelled, and which in its movements conforms to our sense of natural rhythm. We would also expect that it is part of a society in which there are normal preferences as to which kinds of emotion are expressed, which has a practice of helping the distressed in which communication of feeling is possible, and in which there are distinct juvenile and adult phases. We would also expect it

103

to have a face and eyes which are capable of being expressive.

Seven

For any machine which is to be a serious candidate for personhood the qualities that we tend to ascribe to persons and the attitudes that we tend to take towards people must get their application in something close to their paradigm sense. There is no question of a machine being a recipient of our attitudes towards persons for special reasons such as having the right history, or because such attitudes are part of our cultural inheritance or because we are morally obliged to hold such attitudes. It is clear that they do not have the kind of history that we normally expect of persons (being born of woman), nor do we have a cultural inheritance of commonly treating machines of any kind as persons. The moral status of such machines is precisely what is in question. Thus the kinds of thing that will need to be true of any machine that is to be a successful candidate for personhood are the kinds of things that are paradigmatic of persons. A machine which is to be considered a person must be obviously a person since it lacks one of the fundamental features of those cases where the word person normally finds application, namely being born of woman. Thus, for the reasons I have given in this chapter, any machine which is to be considered a person must have a body which amongst other things, is sensitive and vulnerable as a human body is, can express its emotional state through its appearance much as a human can, can walk, run, play, and be childish or adult as a human can, can talk, see, point, and so forth as a human can, and has a repertoire of emotional states similar to a typical human repertoire and much else besides.

These requirements that the machine have, in relevant respects, similar sensual and sensory capacities and possibilities as a human being has, constitute formidable difficulties for any project to build a person. I do not, of course, want to say that any one of these qualities or attributes that I have considered is crucial and that in consequence we cannot coherently conceive of someone who lacked these qualities as a person. Science fiction writers could doubtless contrive some convincing set of circumstances in which someone who had a metal body yet lived would be considered to be fully a person. What I do want to say is that normally with people we do expect them to exhibit all these qualities and attributes and many more. If one of these is missing we may, depending on the circumstances and which quality or attribute is in question, be in doubt about whether the thing in question is a person. What seems certain is that if sufficient of these qualities and attributes are missing then we will be in doubt. Just which combinations of attributes will throw us into doubt in this way will vary with the circumstances and the qualities and attributes which are lacking. If too many are missing then we will surely agree that the thing is not a person. My case to those who would build an artificial person is first, that in order to endow something with one person-like attribute or quality it is almost always necessary to endow it with many others, and second, that for a machine to be a person it must, in its attributes, abilities, and powers, be an exemplar of personhood in all respects other than the one which by definition it lacks, namely, being born of a woman.

Despite this an optimistic person-builder might contend that all I have shown is that there is work to be done, not that it cannot be done. It might be suggested that all that has to be done is to build a machine that fulfils the conditions that I have noted and any further ones of the same kind that might be found by further similar conceptual analyses

Intuitively, I think, one would expect that a machine that had all the necessary capacities that I have discussed would be something like a re-animated corpse. As I commented above (page 81), it is perhaps this intuition that leads Mary Shelly to invoke 'natural electricity' to bring Dr. Frankenstein's monster to life. It is as if having all the right bits', capacities, and richness of possibilities of action were not enough. I think that part of what this intuition is grasping at is the idea that our concept of any particular person requires for its application that that person have *grown* to be as they are. My next chapter will therefore be concerned with analysing our concepts of age and ageing.

Notes

1.   Dennett 1979, p.152.

2.   Pollock 1989, pp.61 - 64.

3.   In simulation a numerical model is created, usually on a computer. In replication prominent physical features of the original object being modelled are reproduced. This distinction is taken from K.M. Sayre.[Sayre 1965]

4.   Miender pp.109 - 113, in *The mind's I: Fantasies and reflections on self and soul* (Ed. Hoffstader and Dennett) 1981.

5 An analysis of some necessary conditions for the ascription of some mental attributes

In this chapter I want to turn the schema I used in the previous chapter around and to take a common bodily attribute (that we grow and thus have a particular kind of history), and to show that it forms part of the background which is crucial under most normal circumstances for the correct ascription of many common mental attributes. If this were to be lacking in a person it would, for conceptual reasons, usually be impossible to have certain attitudes towards them that we normally have towards persons. This makes it very doubtful that a thing which lacked the right kind of body and history (in this sense), could be a person.

One

Suppose we meet someone and talk to them, knowing nothing of their background. We will behave towards them, at least in part, according to how we perceive them. How we perceive a person arises from many things. Amongst these are their style of dress, their mannerisms, and their apparent age. All of these affect our way of behaving towards a person. For example, if a person is very old then they will usually command some kind of deference. The apparent age of a person even affects the manner in which people deviate from such casual behaviour: The manner in which a young person might set about being rude or deliberately disrespectful to an older person is conditioned by their relative ages.

The kind of behaviour which is sometimes called 'looking up towards someone' or 'showing respect for someone', is sometimes manifest by a younger towards an older person. This behaviour consists in, amongst other things, facial expression, bodily posture, not allowing oneself to look bored, not butting in or answering too quickly, indulging their long pauses in speech, and so on. This kind of response might be called a response to 'the gravitas of old age'.

This reaction and form of relating to another is common to all of us. We all do it some of the time. What I want to draw out here is that part of the background which goes with responding to the 'gravitas of old age' is that the person has grown old. It is part of our concept of responding in a manner appropriate to an older person that if someone is responding on this way we will expect the person to whom they are responding to have grown old.

Let us imagine two people responding to one another in conversation. Let us suppose that the first of these two responds to the second with all the mannerisms and behaviour normally displayed before the elderly. If the person to whom the first was responding had the skin, appearance, and demeanour, attire, hair style, and other 'displays' of a person clearly younger than themselves then such a response would seem to be satire, sarcasm, or obsequiousness. Part of what makes a response to someone to be one of respect and not one of obsequiousness is that the person giving the response believes the person to whom the response is given to be the kind of person he finds worthy of respect. In the case we are considering, the kind of respect involved is that due to old age. A crucial part of the context of someone's behaviour which makes that behaviour to be a display of respect for old age and not, for example, obsequiousness, is that the person towards whom the behaviour is directed be old. The philosophical point here is that under normal circumstances, if we believe that the person to whom the response is being given is in fact younger than the person giving the response then we will not understand the response as one of respect. This is part of our concept of what it is to give such a response. Respect of this kind only is that kind of respect against an appropriate background. Our concept of such respect requires this background.

For something which was supposed to be a person, but does not grow, this will pose problems: Part of our concept of a person is that it is the kind of thing which has the capacity to be in relationship to other persons. An object that could not relate to other persons in any way would not be a person whatever its other properties. (This is one reason why a corpse is not a person.) A capacity for relationship of the right kind is crucial for the ascription of personhood in normal cases.

There are, notoriously, examples of persons who seem to lack all capacity for relationship. Anacephalics are one example. Anacephalics have almost no capacity for relationship to other persons at all, nonetheless, most people want to call them persons. In cases like this I believe that a close examination of the way we behave towards them would reveal quite different grounds for treating them as persons to our normal grounds for treating someone as a person. We extend personhood to such cases on grounds of their similarity to paradigm cases. (Part of these grounds will be our knowledge of their history: They were born of women. Part will arise from our notions of duty and morality.) It is important in this context that we could be in doubt as to whether something is a person. Current technology is certainly capable of creating a computer animated replica of an anacephalic that would fool most people. It seems to me that we extend the attribute of personhood to anacephalics because they are just sufficiently similar to paradigm cases of persons for this to make sense. In particular they were born and have grown to be as they are. Against this, the product of a natural abortion early in pregnancy is not usually regarded as a person. Exactly where the line which divides persons from non-persons is drawn is hotly disputed, particularly where termination of a pregnancy is concerned. What seems to me to be important for this essay however, is that there is very widespread agreement about the common, normal, usual, and paradigmatic cases. What I am concerned to demonstrate here is that a feature of our concept of a person in paradigmatic cases is that we believe the person has grown to be as they are.

Let us suppose now that something has been built which resembles a human being in all externally detectable respects except that it never ages or grows old. When any part becomes worn it is replaced by a new one. Thus it is potentially unageing and immortal.

If we know that something does not, in fact, age, then whatever clothes it may wear or demeanour it may adopt or whatever other 'displays' it may give we will not be able to ascribe attitudes to it as we do to humans: For example, if we know that the 'teenager' we see before us is in fact 700 years old we cannot see its 'respectful attitude' to a 50 year old as a respectful attitude (even if we are the 50 year old). The converse is also true. If we know that the aged man we see before us has only been around for 5 days, we cannot see a 'respectful attitude' towards him as respectful. It would seem humorous, mistaken, or sarcastic: Even if we should meet this thing at a time when its displays mimic those of humans of the same age as it really is we will not be able to ascribe attitudes to it as we might do to humans, for we know that it does not age.

This arises from our concept of what it is to be a particular age. Suppose we, or someone else, are confronted with this thing which purports to be a person, displays the demeanour of a very old man, but in fact does not age and is only 5 days old. We would not expect of it the anecdotes of the past, the sense of having lived what is now history, the accumulated experience of life, and so on, that we expect of a genuinely old person. We will thus react and behave towards it in a manner that is different to what we would if we believed it to be a genuinely old person. If a machine should be built so as to exhibit these things (i.e. tell anecdotes etc.), we will regard them and understand them as synthetic, or in some way programmed.

Memories and anecdotes are, usually, told in the first person. If they are not then they are not that person's memories or anecdotes. In consequence a memory or anecdote carries with it, as part of our concept of a memory or anecdote, the idea that the person has been there, or taken part in, or seen, or done those things of which he speaks. Thus if someone remembers when he was in Brazil in the 1950s we will expect him to know what kind of weather that part of Brazil has, that the people in the area he was in have a particular mix of skin colours, that travel in a particular region was, at that time, difficult or easy, and so on. Again, if someone tells an anecdote about walking in the Scottish Highlands then we expect them, at least at that time, to have had legs, to have considered suitable clothing for hill walking at that time (and to be able to tell us about it), to know where the Highlands are, and so forth. We do not expect any of these things of a tape recorder on which memories or anecdotes have been recorded. If we are brought to regard the 'memories' or 'anecdotes' of a machine as synthetic then we will probably consider them as we would the playing of a tape of someone else's memories or anecdotes. Even if the machine was an excellent replica of a person, we would certainly not be prone to react to their memories or anecdotes as anything more meaningful than the ramblings of a psychiatrically diagnosed phantasist who is unsure of what is real and what is phantasy.

Matters would be similar if we were to encounter a machine that gave every appearance of being a teenager but which we know to have been around, behaving as if alive, for 700 years. We would not understand or respect its irreverence and iconoclasm as the irreverence and iconoclasm of youth, for we will know it to be otherwise.

The concept of relating to something that might be a person as the thing that it is, that is to say, in a particular and appropriate fashion, is conceptually connected to its being able to have a particular age and to its being of a particular age. By particular age here I mean such things as infant, child, youth, young man, middle aged, old man, etc. The attitudes that we can understand someone as adopting to an unageing machine are connected and constrained by what we believe to be true about the machine.

Thus, if a machine cannot age as we do it cannot, for conceptual reasons, be understood as taking part in the normal relationship of conversation on the same basis as humans. Its gravitas, or irreverence, or iconoclasm, or whatever would not be accepted for themselves and understood as what they purport to be. They will be seen as synthetic, or as a sham, or as being something different to what they are in humans. (Perhaps we would regard them as an aspect of some kind of natural history' of those machines.) Even when the demeanour and mannerisms happen to be appropriate (by human standards), to the machine's real age, the illusion fostered of genuine irreverence or gravitas and such like will last only until we remind ourselves that this is how it always has been and always will be.

Our concepts of the qualities that a person may display in their public character or demeanour such as gravitas, iconoclasm, or irreverence, are conceptually connected to that person having a particular age: Gravitas in a child is a different concept to gravitas in an old man. Equally, our concepts of our own capacity to relate to something or someone are conceptually connected to that thing being able to have a particular age and to being of a particular age: Nurturing behaviour displayed publicly towards an inanimate object can only be understood by others as meant as some kind of jest, or as radical confusion (as sometimes happens with severe shock). In spite of any other attributes a machine may have, the fact that these machines do not age as we do ensures that we cannot relate to them as we do to humans.

There is a sense in which a machine which did not age as humans do would be outside of life: In so far as life is connected with social life, such a machine would be largely excluded, for our concepts are such as to ensure its exclusion because, as I have shown, they require that that to which they are applied be something that ages. To be outside of life is close to not being alive.

To illustrate this further let us take as an example the celebrating of birthdays. These derive much of their meaning and significance from the way they mark our ageing. In this context the concept of ageing is conceptually connected to the idea of biological ageing. This is crucial to the concept's meaning. If it should transpire that someone thought that humans aged as cans do (rusting and falling to pieces), then he would not have grasped the concept of human ageing. Birthdays do not simply mark the passage of time (although they do that as well) like the striking of a yearly clock. Birthdays mark units on a passage through life, have a typical value range (say, one to ninety), and draw attention to a person's changing biological maturity. This may, in

110

some societies, take the form of formal rites of passage, or it may take the form of changing social expectations upon the individual. (Societies expect different things of adults than they do of children.) These changes are conceptually connected to the concept of having birthdays and to the concept of a particular birthday. In order for such concepts to get application to something it must, among other things, be part of a society. (And this requires very many other things.)

Our concept of what it is to have a birthday leads us to expect that the person (or animal), to which it is applied is the kind of thing that ages biologically and matures. Under most normal circumstances if a thing does not age biologically we cannot truthfully say of it that it is having a birthday and mean by that what we mean when we say it of persons. Further, such a machine could not understand what it is to age as we do: For things that age biologically bodily powers change with age. We get stronger or weaker, eyesight and hearing improve or get worse, speeds of reactions change. These changes result in often irreversible changes in our capacity to act in a manner that is broadly similar for all humans. Such changes would not occur in a machine unless they formed part of the design of that machine. It is a part of our concept of a machine that its components can in principle be repaired or replaced as necessary without limit. Thus there is a lacuna (relative to common human experience) in the experiences which could in principle be available to an experiencing machine. This would show in the things it would do, say, and show understanding of. For example, "I remember when I was a child the Summers were always sunnier." is not something a machine would be prone to say. If someone said this in a conversation which included a machine it would have the effect of cutting the machine out; the machine might then ask for an explanation. In these and similar ways such a machine would be excluded from talk about and celebration of birthdays. Birthdays could not be meaningful for it as they are for us because 'birthday' is conceptually connected to changes in our abilities and bodily powers. Conceptual connections such as these ground the concept of birthdays.

Such changes in abilities and bodily powers result in changes not only to our expectations of a person's abilities which are connected to our concept of a particular birthday and our concept of a person, but also, as the changes happen to us, to our understanding of ourselves. We have a peculiarly close association with our concepts and understanding of ourselves. For example, if we knew someone to be seventy years old but failed to realise that such a person would be unlikely to be able to keep up with people in their twenties when out hill walking then we would be guilty of thoughtlessness and perhaps

111

of being a bit dim. Yet if a person of seventy failed to realise themselves that they would be unlikely to be able to keep up with people in their twenties while out hill walking we would think them either stupid or vain. More generally, if a person persists in trying to do things which we would expect him to know are beyond his bodily powers we would normally think him confused or perhaps a little mad. (Under some abnormal conditions it might be heroic. The conditions, or circumstances are, as usual, crucial.) We expect people to be well informed about their own bodily limitations. To be ignorant, confused, or self-deceived in such matters, particularly as they pertain to common and everyday actions and abilities (such as climbing steps, seeing things at a distance, or hearing clearly) seems very strange, and if it were shown persistently would rapidly lead us to think that person a bit mad.

It is, of course, not surprising that we should have such a close interest and association with the limitations of our abilities and powers and thus of the concepts that they ground, for these may be necessary for our survival. If a machine had powers and abilities quite different from ours we would find that its understanding of itself would be quite different from our understanding of ourselves. In the case of birthdays we can now see that they could not have the same relevance for the machine, in terms of changes in its powers and abilities, as they do for us.

Similar things may be said of ceremonies of passage. Although formal rites of passage are no longer marked so widely or consciously as they once were, the changes in our dispositions that such rites once marked are still very evident. We expect different kinds of behaviour of a child under five years old than we do of a child over five years old. Similarly our expectations of someone change again as they pass fourteen years and as they pass twenty-one years, and so on. This quasi-structural view of human ageing marks and gives form to our dispositions to react to people by age and to our dispositions to expect people to act according to their age.

To react to people as if they were of a particular age is to react to them with the expectation that certain dispositions to behave are typical of people of certain ages. The idea of reacting to people as if they were of a particular age is conceptually connected to people having such age typical dispositions. The possibility of having such age-typical dispositions, such as wetting of nappies in infants, rebellion in adolescents, and conservatism in old age, depends on human biological processes and on the structures and expectations of our society. (Changes in bodily powers with age are substantially biologically determined, and phenomena such as adolescent rebellion are not usual in some

112

societies which initiate young men into war-bands or hunting groups at this age and initiate young women into groups where they are prepared for marriage.)

The concept of eighteenth birthdays, twenty-first birthdays, the advent of manhood or womanhood and so on are conceptually connected to ageing. These concepts would not normally get application to something which did not age as we do. Such machines would be excluded from being understood in this way, that is, as passing through life . Thus there are a range of attitudes which are important to our concept of a person that we may have towards persons which we cannot have towards such machines.

Machines which do not age biologically would also lack some aspects of the sense of a personal past and future that we have. Thus the notion of retirement could not conjure up the same hopes, fears, and expectations, that they do for a human because machines would have at retirement much the same powers and limitations of 'body' and 'mind' (assuming an adequate supply of spare parts), as they do at 'birth'. This would result in their speaking differently on the subject and providing for the future in different ways. (They would probably get more generous life insurance terms as well.) In this way such machines would display an understanding of the world which was characterised by things having relative degrees of importance and significance in their lives which would always seem quite alien to us.

The sense of such being outside of 'life' would be further reinforced by their concepts about themselves being significantly different to our analogous concepts. Their understanding of age and ageing would affect their dispositions to act in a different way to the way ours affect us. For them the concept of ageing would have significantly different conceptual connections.

Similar considerations apply to the concept of childhood with such machines. If such a machine is created as a child then it remains a child for as long as it exists. Such a 'child' is not the kind of thing which will one day be an adult. They can never 'be the future'. 'Childhood' for such a machine would not be something in their past that they once inhabited, rather it would be a condition of some machines which would be as alien to one of the machines that was created an 'adult' as would be the condition of being an Ostrich.

The concept of childhood is conceptually connected to the fact that children age and grow into adults. The concept could not normally get application to such machines. In contrast it is part of our normal repertoire of possible attitudes towards a person that we may regard them as a child, and it is part of our concept of a person that we understand them as having been a child.

For such machines it would make no sense for them to be nostalgic about childhood or to regard it as a time when the world seemed magical. They could only speak about it as a condition they had observed in others. They could never truthfully speak of it as something they had experienced. Thus the understanding of childhood that they could manifest would be different from ours, and this would show in their speech. Again this would make them seem to be outside of the normal flow of life.

Many other examples could be found. For example, one of these machines that is not a teenager would never have been a teenager and would never have had those attitudes and dispositions to respond which are characteristic of teenagers.

What we have found from this analysis of the concept of ageing is that a machine that was like a human in all externally detectable respects except that it did not age, would, for conceptual reasons, not be treated as a normal person but, on account of its not ageing, as something apart. It could not be understood as having birthdays or viewing old age or childhood as we do. It could not, for conceptual reasons, understand ageing, growing up, childhood, birthdays, and ceremonies of passage, with respect to itself as we do with respect to ourselves. This would show in its behaviour, concerns, attitudes, and conversations.

These lacuna in its understanding and capacities are far from being small or insignificant. Such a machine cannot be the subject of certain attitudes, even in principle. It cannot be seen to be taking part in life as we do. It cannot be seen to be on a road leading from childhood to old age. It cannot be seen to be the kind of thing that of its nature is likely to gain in wisdom with the passage of years (even if, as it happens, it does). This is because these are all things which are conceptually connected to ageing. In this way such a machine would seem somehow to be outside of 'life', or not taking part in 'life', or not really 'alive as we are'. This by itself would, I think, put most people in doubt some of the time as to whether to treat it as a person.

It might be suggested that if such things were common we would simply change our concepts. Doubtless if such machines were common we would develop new concepts to apply to them, but to change our present concepts and to use them consistently with both humans and machines would result in whole continents of our presently known meanings shifting or submerging.

That we do grow and age is a background fact of life that is true of everyone. It is only in virtue of having such a background that many of our social activities are indeed what they are. The suggestion that

114

all this might change is the suggestion that we might develop a language in which ageing did not form part of the background to many of the words and concepts of the language. But the fact that we age is incorrigibly prior to language. We cannot chose to make ageing less important to us. Our concepts in these matters are forged by the interaction between the way the world is and the way that we are.

Thus any change to our concepts so that they did not go with a background which included the fact that we age would involve changing our concepts so that whether the subject to whom we applied them aged or not was irrelevant to whether their application was correct or appropriate. Thus in such a world 'child' would apply with exactly the same meaning to human children as to machines created as children. 'Birthday' would apply with identical meaning to the marking of a year's passage both to humans and to unageing machines. The way in which we judge whether certain behaviour to another is respectful, sarcastic, or obsequious, would have nothing to do with the relative ages of the participants, and so on. I am not sure that such a world can be imagined coherently, but if it ca then in such a world 'children' would not be children, 'grannies' would not be grannies, 'teenagers' would not be teenagers, 'birthdays' would not be birthdays, 'old age' would not be old age, 'childhood' would not be childhood, 'rites of passage' would not be rites of passage, 'acting your age' would not be acting your age, 'respectful', 'iconoclastic', 'irreverent', 'obsequious', 'sarcastic', or 'satirical' demeanour would not be respectful, or iconoclastic, or irreverent, or obsequious, or sarcastic, or satirical demeanour and so on. In short, under such circumstances our human world would have changed utterly.

It is therefore certain that we would be unable to regard such machines as we regard a person or have an attitude towards such machines as we have towards persons if the machine was like us in most relevant respects but did not age in a relevantly similar manner to the way we do. Such a machine would naturally be excluded by our attitudes from many of our social activities. For such machines birthdays, ceremonies of passage and such like things, if they had them, could not play the same roles in their 'lives' as they do in ours.

Thus at the very least we would be prone to regard such machines as having a very different life to what we do and would probably be prone to doubt that they 'really lived', as we do, at all. It seems then that if something does not age biologically this alone will throw considerable doubt on whether we would regard it as a person. Put the other way round: If an artificial person is ever to be built it will need to be the kind of thing that ages in a relevantly similar manner to the way we do. This does not simply mean, be the kind of thing that wears out, but rather be the kind of thing that so changes with time that others relate to it and it is constrained to relate to others in a manner which gives it a characteristic demeanour for each of its different periods of life and would lead people to think of it as increasing in wisdom and maturity. This might be expressed by saying that it must be something to which the metaphor of a path of life would naturally get application in some similar sense to the sense it has when applied to humans.

Two

Having concluded that it is necessary for the application of our concept 'person' that a thing age in an appropriate fashion it seems worth enquiring how similar its history must be to a human history if it is to be a person. I have already touched on this briefly above (page 90). The basic thought is that if something ages as humans do then it has a certain kind of history and certain expectations of the future.

A human history includes such things as having human parents, being born of woman, having started life as an infant during which time one was helpless and needed to be nurtured, having a childhood, and so on. Such a history is part of the unquestioned background which we expect to be present when we use many of our concepts which apply to persons. We have seen in the discussion of ageing above that a normal human history forms part of the grounds for the application of many of the concepts which normally we would expect to be able to apply to persons.

When, as sometimes happens with problem cases like anacephalics, very severe deformity, and late abortions, the moral status of something with respect to personhood is brought into question, appeal to the thing's history, whether implicit or explicit, forms a crucial part of the discussion. If an anacephalic had not been born of a woman but had been built then it certainly would not be a person. If it should be that all other things built by the same process were persons then this one would be a 'reject' or a 'second' or a result of a problem in the building process. The lack of the right kind of history would ensure that the notion of an artificial anacephalic being a person would not be taken seriously. An artificial late aborted foetus is not a person, not even a dead one. In the case of severe deformity (such as 'the elephant man'),

116

it is the appeal to other human qualities that convinces us that it is, in fact, a person. This is not a matter of prejudice, but a matter of where we are willing to apply the concept 'person'. Artificial anacephalics and artificial late aborted foetuses are not the kinds of things that could meaningfully be described as a person.

To put the same point more generally; if something is a person then we have many expectations about it, and amongst those expectations is a very strong one that it should have the right kind of history. It must have grown, in a manner very similar to human growth, to be as it is. Details, such as being born of an incubator rather than a woman, might be changed in such a history without undermining our willingness to call a thing a person. If such details of a things history are unusual and it is still to be thought of as a person then it must in most other respects exhibit features that are paradigms of the features we would expect to be exhibited by a person. If it does not do so then English speakers will feel unwilling to apply the word 'person' to it in the same sense as it would be applied to a human. This difference in sense would show in the way that the thing was treated.

For this reason it would not be sufficient to make us willing to call a machine a person if the machine were created with a mature human body. In particular it is false to suppose that if a machine is created with a mature human body and a computer in its head that, if the program is appropriate, it will necessarily be caused to behave in all observable respects exactly like a person. If a machine is to be a person then, because it is not born of a woman, it must, in the ways that I have discussed (and many more beside), have an appropriate history and be very like a human indeed.

6 Emotions, angels and extra-terrestrials

The account of when something is a person that I am adumbrating seems to beg the question of how we would recognise an emotion such as joy in a martian or other extra-terrestrial. It might appear from the way my argument is going that it is likely not only to deny personhood to all machines but to all non-human life-forms as well. This has been characterised for me by Professor R. Sharpe as 'cosmic racism'.

Much of what we would be prepared to say of an extra-terrestrial would be tied to the details of the case. To say, intelligibly, that something is feeling joy requires that its body be of an appropriate form. It makes sense to talk about a joyful dog, but not about a joyful oyster. Oysters do not have those possibilities of action which are necessary for the display of joy.

If the martian's body was quite unlike ours, yet it appeared to exhibit social behaviour like ours, we would probably not know what to say. Our language and experience do not extend to coping with such things. Here we would have reached the limit of our current language.

It is only in the case of the martian having an appropriate kind of body and behaving in a manner that we would call appropriate that we will be prepared to say that it is exhibiting joy. The requirement for us to be able to say truthfully that the martian is a person will be similar. We must be able to recognise its body as appropriately like that of a person.

Similar problems may be raised with angels: It is not clear whether there are angels, but there is a strong tradition that if there are, then they are persons. If my analysis of circumstances where we can and cannot apply the word 'person' meaningfully excludes angels a priori then many people would say that I have drawn the boundaries much too tightly.

To me it seems that we do not have sufficient experience of dealing with angels to know what to say. Usually they are depicted with a human-like form which suggests that many of our normal concepts

118

which we expect to apply to persons (hunger, hope, fear, love etc.) might well get application to an angel. The problem here is not one of how to describe an angel if one were to see one, but, so to speak, what to do if one comes round to tea.

What I think we can say is that if our normal social experience should come to include meeting angels quite often then our concept 'person' would change in its usage to include them. It would then be important that the constraints on our willingness to apply the concept 'person' should not be so changed as to allow in anything that is clearly not a person. Put this way, we can now see that there could be no danger of that happening as the source of change is a recognition of something that is obviously a person anyway. Thus, if we ever should come to mix with angels our concept of person (and our language generally) will stretch in a natural fashion to accommodate our new experiences and way of life.

7 Some limits to functionalist accounts of persons

I believe that so far in this essay I have shown that anything that is to be a candidate for personhood must have a body that closely resembles a human body in its form, that is sensitive to its environment in a similar fashion to a human body, that grows and ages with an infancy and childhood as humans do, and that has a relevantly similar history to a human history. This candidate for personhood sounds very like a human being. This is not surprising. Our concept of a person has been forged by a society of humans with humans as exemplars of personhood.

Four of the authors I have chosen to criticise are concerned at some level with truth and logic. For Putnam and the early Dennett truth functional logic plays a normative role in their thought. The systematic determination of meaningfulness of sentences is to be achieved through assimilating normal language to effectively computable formulae in a logical system. Pylyshyn, approaching questions with the perspective of a computer scientist, seems to assume that meaning in language is effectively computable. Fodor dismisses Wittgenstein as beyond his comprehension on the grounds that Wittgensteinians will not submit themselves to logically necessary and sufficient conditions for the meaningfulness of a word[1] Having thus excused himself from the trouble of discussing truth and logic Fodor goes on to write as if truth functional logic was beyond question. Each of these authors is a functionalist in the sense put forward by Block in his paper *Troubles with functionalism*.[2]

In the light of this, we need some kind of explanation as to where functionalist accounts of persons (which normally admit the possibility of person building in principle) have gone wrong. I do not propose to mount a full analysis and critique of functionalism here, but to point to where I think it may have gone astray.

The term functionalism covers many different theories. Block characterises functionalism as the thesis that:

Each type of mental state is a state consisting in a disposition to act in certain ways *and to have certain mental states*, given certain sensory inputs and certain mental states.[Block, N.J. (1978), p.262, His emphasis.]

K.V. Wilkes in *Functionalism, Psychology, and the philosophy of Mind*[3] has pointed out that the applicability of a particular function to some structure depends on the nature of the structure; to be able to pick something up a machine must have an arm and a hand. Functionalism is therefore not truly structure independent. Wilkes also points out[4] that even with suitable structures functional isomorphism may be uninteresting. Both men and machines may wash clothes by soaping, soaking, rinsing, and drying them. This does not help to provide a description of men in terms of machines.

Despite such basic problems (and Wilkes raises further problems in the same paper) with getting a detailed and specific functional theory of mind off the ground, it can, with a bit of hand waving, still seem to be a plausible route to a theoretical account of mental states which could provide the theoretical background for a project to build a person. John Pollock,[5] uses functionalism in exactly this way. Thus with 'suitable' structures $S_1, S_2,...,S_n$ and a theory T of mental states (assuming such is possible), Pollock[6] characterises functionalism as follows:

For a functional theory T and states $S_1, S_2,...,S_n$

$$T(S_1, S_2,...,S_n)$$

describes the functional behaviour of the system consisting of $S_1, S_2,...,S_n$. The functional 'behaviour' means the manner in which the elements $S_1, S_2,...,S_n$ affect each other and the overall behaviour of the system described in functional language. That is to say, what the system does.

Such a functional theory relates structures and function. Anything that has the right structure will conform to the functional theory $T(X_1, X_2,...,X_n)$ where X_i is a variable.

Pollock suggests[7] that such a theory T will be true for persons only if:

(1) The functions described are all of those and only those that we expect of persons.

(2) The values which the structural variables $(X_1, X_2,...,X_n)$ may take are defined in such a manner as to include all those found in known persons.

(3) The relationship between $(S_1, S_2,...,S_n)$ and the functional behaviour described by T does in fact obtain in known persons.

To me it seems that a theory T which conformed to any of these conditions could never be constructed. Concerning (1) it seems to me that the possibilities of action that we have are such that new expressions, feelings, and ways of life can always emerge. Thus if this functional description T is to describe all functions that we expect of humans it will always be incomplete.

For any project to build a machine which conforms to a disposition given by some theory T, the fact that the theory must always be incomplete renders the project impossible. The openness of the future, its possibilities, ensure that this route to person building is closed.

Concerning point (2) I have already argued (in chapter 4), that any structures that are to be persons must resemble humans very closely both in their structure and in their history. I have noted above (page 42, also [8]), that Pollock considers this no more important than whether a can opener is made of steel or aluminium.

The very close connection I have demonstrated between body form, details of body structure, and personhood, shows that the values that the variable $(X_1, X_2,...,X_n)$ may take are all ones that we would normally be prone to describe as 'much the same'. That is to say that the close dependence of personhood on the human form will render any insights that a successful functional theory might offer uninteresting, at least to a would-be person builder. Thus the insights that a detailed, successful, functional theory of personhood might be able to offer could be no more than such observations as things like live human bodies with human histories tend to behave like 'persons'. This makes the project to find a true functional account of persons seem something of a red herring. Certainly it does not offer a route to person building remotely like that imagined by enthusiasts for the computer metaphor.

Concerning (3) (and obliquely (1)) I have argued and shall argue further that what makes some particular functional behaviour described by T to be the behaviour that it is, is in large part the human context of the behaviour and the person's past. Such context is crucial to the conceptual distinction between shamming anger, real anger, and some kind of madness that appears like anger. In particular I wish to draw out that what makes it true that the relationship between some structures $(S_1, S_2,...,S_n)$ and the functional behaviour described by some theory T is indeed the relationship that it is, is that the behaviour takes place in a particular context. That context must include being part of a society of persons. To see this, let us return to some points raised by Wittgenstein.[9]

One of Wittgenstein's constant concerns is to draw our attention away from purely theoretical or abstract notions and towards what real people in real situations actually do and say. Wittgenstein discusses at one point[10] how we in our society go about measuring the length of a table. Here I want to apply his insights to the question 'When is it true that a table is 3 feet long?'. I want to say that the answer to this must be consistent with answers to the more basic question 'How would people in our society go about resolving a disagreement about the actual length of a particular table?'. The answer is surely that they would measure it. This obvious answer hides a mass of important detail.

Wittgenstein points out that if one of the parties were to measure the table with an elastic tape measure or with a ruler that expanded visibly with slight changes in temperature this would not resolve the disagreement, for the activity of which this was a part would not be what we call measuring. What we mean by measuring in such a context is a particular practice carried out in a particular way.

The importance of this statement of the obvious is that it is simple and could be reworked for any disagreement about how the world is for which the suggestion 'Well lets find out.' could in principle provide a solution. What it suggests, queer as it may sound, is that we must have some kind of agreement in our practices before agreement and disagreement about the way the world is can get started. Measuring is a practice that we have in our society and that may be performed correctly or incorrectly. What we mean by measuring, or at least, measuring correctly, in any particular circumstance involves acting in the right way. If someone does not act in the right way, has for example, a deviant practice for measuring, then we will say of what they are doing that that is not what we mean by measuring. This is not simply a felicitous turn of phrase, it is quite literally so: If a person sets about (as they would say) measuring something in a fashion that does not correspond to our idea of what is involved in going about measuring that thing in those circumstances then what they are doing is not what we call 'measuring'. In this way the meaning of some words can be seen to be inseparably linked to actions and practices. This is part of what Wittgenstein meant when he wrote quoting Goethe's Faust "in the beginning was the deed". [11] Thus a claim that a table is 3 feet long only becomes capable of being true or false in the context of an agreed practice of measuring and any meaningful claim that it is true that some table is 3 feet long must take account of the practice of measuring of the society of speakers of that language.

The significance of all this for this essay is that such actions are conceptually prior to the words and sentences whose meaning they help to ground. To see this let us take an example:

A gesture which means 'go and fetch some water' must be understood by both the person giving the order and the person receiving the order as meaning the same thing before the question of whether the order has been obeyed can arise. The crucial test of whether they do understand the same thing will lie in the actions of the one who receives the order. Does he, or does he not, do what is expected of him, that is, fetch some water? If he does not fetch some water then either he has disobeyed, or he has not understood the gesture correctly. Not to understand the gesture correctly is to understand the gesture as meaning something else or not to recognise the gesture as the gesture that it is.

What 'something else' amounts to here is to understand the gesture (that is, to find it meaningful), but not in the fashion intended by the person who made the gesture. Perhaps the person to whom the gesture was made fetches a spade instead of some water. He will then have acted other than the person making the gesture intended him to act. The actions that would have been what the person making the gesture meant by the gesture, (lowering the bucket into the well, pulling it out full of water, etc.) are not the same as those which the person to whom the gesture was made understands as the meaning of the gesture. The 'agreement in action' which forms the grounds of the mutually understood meaning of the gesture, is lacking. In this particular case the 'agreement in action' (or lack of it), need not be some kind of identity or similarity of action which is performed by both the persons, but what is meant by that gesture in that context. These observations seem to me to hold true even if the person in question could not read, write, or even speak.

The kind of 'agreement' which I am considering here seems very basic and the grounds of the possibility of communication within a society. Without it there would be no possibility of meaningful discourse or instruction. I do not want to say that a single failure to understand gesturing, or a single mistaken interpretation of a gesture undermines the possibility of meaning for a society, nor that multiple failures of this kind would do so. What I am concerned to point out here is that behind every such successful request or ordering by gesture lies this kind of agreement in action. The combination of all these 'agreements' form part of the grounds of the possibility of meaning. (This is not to suggest that these 'agreements' can be arbitrary.) My point here is simply that while there can be meaning and successful communication without verbal language, there cannot be mutually agreed meaning, and thus communication without this kind of 'agreement in action'. [12]

These considerations suggest strongly that the agglomerate of such 'agreements in action' form part of the grounds of the possibility of meaningful speech. Without the mass of agreements of this kind which permeate daily life communication would cease and meaning would fail, for the sounds that make up speech and the letters that make up words would have lost their meaningful connections to the world. [13]

Since this account of the grounds of the possibility of meaning is not a logical deduction but rather a collection of observations, the only way to generalise it is by a dialectical exposition. This I propose to do by considering two apparently difficult cases and showing that even there 'agreement in action' can be seen to form a crucial part of the grounds of the possibility of meaning.

The first case I want to consider is what, on this analysis, is the difference between shamming anger and really being angry. The answer to this may well be nothing, in the sense of nothing that we could ever realistically know about. We can, after all, be fooled quite easily by someone shamming anger and never know that we have been fooled. What I hope to show therefore is not that there will always be a difference in actions between someone shamming anger and someone who really is angry, but that these two things are conceptually different and that these concepts and their differences can be seen to have their meaning grounded in actions or dispositions to act.

Exactly what the difference in actions will be will differ from case to case, however, we can find some broad generalisations: Anger is susceptible to explanation; it has reasons. If it is true that a person is angry then there will be something, an event or state of affairs, which he may cite as a reason for anger if we knew enough about the person who was made angry and their circumstances. A state of mind or an emotion in somebody which appeared to be anger but of which we learned that there was no explanatory reason and which was not a case of shamming anger would surely appear to be something like madness.

On the other hand, with shamming, there is no such reason for the anger, for if there were such a reason then it would not be shamming. To sham anger is something that one can decide to do voluntarily. Thus even if we imagine that two people have identical immediate past histories, and thus both have experienced the same events (let us suppose that they have just had an encounter with a rude and unhelpful petrol-pump attendant), it may still be true that one of them gets genuinely angry at the encounter while the other (possible for some quite unrelated reason), does not, but decides to sham anger. For the one who is genuinely angry the encounter with the petrol pump attendant will be a reason for his anger whereas for the one shamming anger it will not (for he is shamming anger).

From this we can see that a mass of (possibly counterfactual), hypotheticals about how these people would be disposed to act if certain circumstances held will be true in virtue of this state of affairs. In particular there will be true hypotheticals about the dispositions of these people to act which are true of one and not of the other, and thus could reveal the differences in their mental states. What I want to say is that these true hypotheticals are, for each of these words, articulations of the meanings of these words. These differences are then differences in dispositions to act if certain circumstances should hold. It is in virtue of the truth of these hypotheticals that it is true that one man is angry and the other shamming anger. The difference between the two is to be found in the hypotheticals which are true for one case but not the other. This difference is manifested and grounded in their different dispositions to act. Whatever account of truth or emotional states one may hold there will be such distinguishing hypotheticals, the absence of which would throw doubt on the truth of the ascription of the mental state.

Thus, what makes it true that a person is angry or that a person is shamming anger is their dispositions to act. The difference between these two mental states consists in differences in these dispositions. This analysis has shown that our concepts of anger and of shamming anger are such that there must be such differences of dispositions, whatever one's account of truth, for these differences of dispositions are part of what we mean by anger and shamming anger. They are therefore something of which any account of the truth of sentences ascribing anger or the shamming of anger must take account. Further, the very possibility of there being a distinction between sham anger and real anger must, on this analysis, depend on there being 'prior agreement' on the meaning of actions.

If we return now, for my second example, to my question (page 123), 'When is it true that a table is 3 feet long?' we can see that the answer 'When we find it to be 3 feet long by measuring it.', requires that we (who would answer the question) have common, so to speak 'agreed', practices of measuring. This requires that we can agree that the actions and practices by which the table is measured on different occasions are the same. This sameness can be seen to be relative to our interests which ultimately depend on the role that measuring plays in our lives. To see this, I want to consider the question 'When is it true to say that a table is 3 feet long?' in more detail.

There are many ways of measuring (indeed theory of mensuration can form an entire university degree course). If it is indeed true, as I maintain, that there need be nothing common to all cases of measuring the table, then I need to explain exactly how it comes about that those actions of measuring can sensibly be described as 'the same' (because

126

they are all cases of measuring), yet, at the same time within the same account, 'different' (because they are each examples of different techniques of measuring).

On this account, words, sentences, gestures, and the like will have the same meaning if the actions which ground their meanings are the same. If two people understand the verb 'to measure' (in a particular context), in the same way then they will measure a particular thing, in that context, in the same way. Similarly, if two people understand the gesture discussed above as having the same meaning and are obedient they will both respond to the gesture by fetching some water. I want to say the they will act in the same way. For these examples at least, sameness of meaning is founded in sameness of action.

What now needs to be explained is what makes two actions the same. Actions in many (but not all), circumstances bare some resemblance to tools in that they have a purpose which is to achieve a certain end. Tools are often said to be of the same type if they serve the same purpose, that is to say, will serve just as well as another of that type. Thus what is necessary for a tool's inclusion under the heading 'spade' is that it can serve as a spade. What I want to say is that it is the role that an action plays in a person's life (somewhat like the purpose that a tool may serve) that gives it the meaning that it has for him. Similarly it is the role that an action plays in the life of a society that gives it the meaning that it has for that society.

It seems to me that there is little reason to suppose that the notion of role in a person's or a society's life can be given precise definition, - natural language and life are not that tidy. Rather there are reasons to suppose the reverse: What gets included under a particular description is not only governed by the qualities of the thing and the role that it can play in the language user's life but is also governed by a certain degree of arbitrariness which simply reflects the way we, or the society of language users, are at that time. Wittgenstein draws attention[14] to the way we judge resemblance within a family (for example resemblance of facial features). Two members of a family may have the same nose, two the same mouth, two the same eyes, and there may be no single feature common to all. Nonetheless, in most cases, we will be able to agree amongst ourselves that there is indeed a likeness in their faces. Further, there is no reason to suppose that there is some logical disjunction of facial features, one or more of which must be similar between two members of a family for us to be prone to say that there is a family likeness. What we see as similar may be some facial mannerism, for example, a twitch or characteristic movement of the head.

Computer metaphor enthusiasts, particularly Fodor, might insist here that the catalogue of qualities in virtue of which we make such judgements of likeness must be finite and that therefore it is possible in principle to give a finite disjunction of features one or more of which will be common to any two faces in which we can see a family likeness. This position seems to me to be flawed for two reasons: First there would seem to be no explanation for why some other faces which are not members of the family yet have some of the relevant features in common with one member of the family should be excluded. We do tend to agree on such exclusions. Second the hypothesis of a logical disjunction underlying such judgements would deprive the explanation of its explanatory power without replacing it by means of the hypothesis. The hypothesised disjunction does not of itself explain. It is merely a cataloguing of how we behave. It is as if each new similarity feature were to be added to the catalogue as it was found. Such an explanation ceases to give any account of why we judge family likeness to extend as far as we do and judge it to end where we do. As Wittgenstein comments[15] such an hypothesis is only a play with words. It is similar to saying that there is something that runs through the whole of a thread; namely the continuous overlapping of the fibres.

The explanation that I want to give of this is not that it is arbitrary but simply that it reflects the way we are. Our judgements in these things may change with time, with our interests, be swayed by circumstances and the opinions of others, and even vary with our mood. All that is needed is that our judgements of similarity be sufficiently constant to allow our normal life to proceed unhindered. In some cases what leads us to judge that two actions, or sets of actions, or qualities, are the same may be expressible by fairly precise conditions and restrictions; for example, what makes two actions both to be ones of fetching some water. In other cases the conditions and restrictions we can give may be much looser; for example, the judgement of family resemblance in faces. What seems to determine the matter are our interests, what is at stake for us collectively or individually in the outcome of the activity in question.

Judgements of sameness of actions and thus of sameness of measuring must therefore be relative to our interests. They amount to judgements that in those contexts the actions in questions play for us the same roles in our lives. Thus the 'agreement in actions' that I want to say is part of the grounds of the possibility of meaning (and therefore of the grounds of the truth of 'This table is 3 feet long'), requires that our interests and ways of life be sufficiently similar for it to be possible that these actions of measuring play the same role for all of us.

This appears to pose a problem as there are many different practices of measuring and any one practice will involve the deployment of various different techniques none of which need be common to all instances of measuring. The notion of sameness of role needs to be spelled out more clearly.

One practice of measuring involves the deployment of such techniques as laying a tape measure along a table correctly, reading it correctly, aligning the end of the tape with the end of the table, and so on. This practice of measuring lengths is conceptually connected to these techniques. By this I mean that if we say of someone that they understand or have grasped the concept of, measuring a table in this fashion, then it is a part of what we mean by that that they will have grasped other connected concepts and will be able to demonstrate connected techniques. Which concepts and which techniques will vary between individuals. We may want to say that two people have grasped the concept of measuring a table, and do so on the grounds that they have demonstrated knowledge of appropriate connected concepts and have exhibited connected techniques and practices. The repertoire of concepts, techniques and practices that they have demonstrated or exhibited may be different and we may even find that their respective repertoires have only a small degree of overlap. There need not be any single concept or technique which is common to all people who have grasped the concept to measuring a table; rather, as in the case of family resemblance, it is enough that we are able agree. What is important is whether they can do what we expect a person who has grasped the concept of measuring to be able to do. One consequence of this view is that there are bound to be borderline cases where we will not be able to agree with each other as to whether a person has grasped the concept of measuring a table or not; and this is what we find in the world.

This account needs some illustration: If there was disagreement as to whether each of two people (say a physicist and a carpenter) had grasped the concept of measuring a table, we would expect to be able to decide whether each of them had grasped the concept or not.

We might expect the carpenter to be able to use a tape measure and to measure the table. We would expect him to be able to read the tape correctly. We would expect him to lay the tape along a long side of the table and not, for instance, diagonally. We might expect the carpenter to be able to calculate the length of two of the tables put end to end, or be able to tell us whether the table would fit, broad side on, through a doorway he had previously measured. We might expect him to be able to tell from the measurements whether a particular piece of wood would be long enough for making another similar table, and so on. In short, we would expect him to demonstrate those abilities and capacities that go with having grasped the concept of measuring the length of a table.

Each of these examples of techniques, practices, and knowledge would help to convince us that the carpenter had grasped the concept of measuring the length of a table, however, any one of them could be absent without destroying our belief that the carpenter had grasped the concept of measuring the length of a table. For example, if it transpired that this carpenter had always measured with a ruler, never having come across a tape measure before, we might be surprised but if he could exhibit other relevant knowledge, techniques, and practices, we would surely be happy to say that he had grasped the concept of measuring the length of a table. If the carpenter was blind or extremely short sighted and needed an assistant to read the tape for him this, by itself, would not lead us to say that he had not grasped the concept of measuring the length of a table. An inability to calculate the sum or product of two numbers would not lead us to say that the carpenter had not grasped the concept of measuring the length of a table, particularly of it turned out that the carpenter had some rule of thumb or set of tables which allowed him to draw the necessary practical conclusions with adequate reliability for his purposes. The same may be said of being able to tell whether a table would fit through a particular doorway or whether a piece of wood would be big enough for making a similar table. In short none of these techniques, practices, and knowledge are crucial to the concept of measuring the length of a table. It is the possession of an adequate number of such skills or techniques that is crucial. If the carpenter can exhibit an adequate number of relevant techniques, practices, and knowledge we will certainly be convinced that he has grasped the concept of measuring the length of a table.

The important point here is that there is no reason to believe that behind these techniques and practices lies an abstract something (perhaps a vastly complex logical formula with suitable definitions) which plays the role of a kind of essence of table measuring and in virtue of some kind of agreement with which we say that the carpenter has grasped the concept of measuring a table. This attitude which regards these techniques and practices as symptoms of some underlying (invisible), structural, quality is a demand for something to which we may point and say that that is what is crucial to the grasp of this ability and that it is in virtue of that structural quality that we ascribe that ability. Yet there is no sign of this 'something'. We ascribe a grasp of the concept of measuring on the basis of whether the person can do the

130

job, the rest is a problem-causing supposition which can point to little for its justification: There need not be any one thing that is crucial upon which the ascription of a concept depends.

At the start of this example I introduced two people, a carpenter and a physicist (nothing important hangs on their professions), because it seems to me that we might ascribe a grasp of the concept of measuring the length of a table to each of them on quite different grounds. Perhaps the physicist is quadriplegic and unable to use any measuring device. We might find that the physicist was able to give a lucid account of the mathematical concept of measure and its relationship to our concept of space. We might find that he could instruct us how to program a computer to model a table and display it on a monitor, to be able to calculate if it would float and other things. In such a case we would surely want to say that this person had grasped the concept of measuring the length of a table, even though he might not be able to measure a table and had never in fact done so.

The grounds for ascribing a grasp of the concept of measuring the length of a table to a physicist may have no overlap with the grounds in the case of a carpenter (or any two people from any other professions). What convinces us that they have grasped the concept is not some crucial thing, or a disjunction of things that can be crucial, but that these people, in their contexts, can do the sorts of things which we expect of someone who has grasped the concept of measuring the length of a table.

The role of context here is important, for the addition of a single further detail can transform our perception of what is going on and thus our willingness to ascribe a grasp of the concept. For example, suppose that all the techniques, practices, and knowledge which I described above in discussing the carpenter turned out to have been exhibited at the time when we observed them as part of an obscure religious ritual (perhaps neo-pythagorean), would we not ask for further evidence before we were willing to ascribe a grasp of the concept of measuring a table? More generally, it seems it is always possible that we shall find that we were mistaken. [16]

This example seems to me to illustrate the way that conceptual connections and contexts form the grounds for our ascription of meaning. The example also seems to me to suggest that these kinds of consideration about truth and sameness may be applied quite generally. There need not be any one thing in virtue of which we ascribe some ability, concept, or understanding to a person. What is crucial is that we believe that they are capable of doing those things which exhibit the ability or possession of the concept in question. This example also brings out the way in which language and meaning in language is like a vast web whose threads are conceptual connections. [17]

From these considerations it seems to me that what makes it true that the table is 3 feet long is that when we measure it we find it to be 3 feet long. What is common to all techniques of measuring the length of a table is that they inform us of the length of the table. These simple claims however can now be seen to conceal ramifications which can touch any area of our life which is connected with or affected by the practice of measuring.

If we return now to Pollock's 3rd condition for a true functionalist description of persons (discussed above page 122), we can see that the behaviour in question is individuated by its social and environmental context. Thus it might be that on no two occasions of some behaviour (say thinking about my job), that the same structures (S_i) were involved. So any notion of a constant relationship between the structural constants $(S_1, S_2, ...,S_n)$ and the behaviour described by T would be vacuous. The answer to the question 'What, on a true functionalist account, is common to all cases of my thinking about my job?' may well be nothing, (except that I am thinking about my job).

From the foregoing account of truth and sameness we can see that there is no reason to believe that behaviour can be individuated by its function in any fashion that could be of use for a functionalist theory of mind, and we have seen some reasons for believing that it cannot. Consequently it is unlikely that Pollock's brand of functionalism or anything remotely like it will be able to provide an account of what it is to think about my job or many other aspects of the life of persons. It therefore seems unlikely that functionalism can provide a route to person building.

Notes

1.   Fodor, Jerry, A. (1976), pp.2-3.

2.   Block, N.J. (1978), pp261-325.

3.   Wilkes, K.V. pp.147-167.

4.   ibid. p.157.

5.   Pollock, John, L. (1989), pp.61-68.

6.   ibid. Loc.Cit.

7.   ibid. Loc. Cit.

8.   ibid. p.61.

9.   The ideas in this chapter owe much to a paper *Im Anfang war die Tat.*, by

Peter Winch in *Perspectives on Wittgenstein* edited by Irving Bloch. Pub: Oxford, Blackwell 1981. -Papers from the Wittgenstein colloquuium 1976, London Ont.

10.   Wittgenstein, Ludwig, (1974).

11.   Wittgenstein, Ludwig, (Philosophia, vol. 66, pp420).

12.   This brief account skates over many ancient problems in the philosophy of mind. Notorious amongst these is the objection that admits all that I have written but continues that while all that I have written may be true, still the real nature (the essence, if you like) of meaning is to be found standing behind the words in the attitude, will, and intentions of the speaker or person making the gesture.

Such an objection begs questions about the status of meaning and its vulnerability to radical sceptical objections which seek to drive a wedge between actions and their meanings.

13.   I have not demonstrated that meaning must be grounded in actions, merely that the idea is very plausible. To demonstrate that it is grounded in actions would require a lengthy digression on the meaning, relevance, possibility, and coherence of private languages.

14.   Wittgenstein, Ludwig, (1981), §67.

15.   ibid, §67.

16.   This seems endlessly possible in life. I heard it reported that in some cases when a man dies and it turns out that unknown to his wife he had a mistress for many years that the widow suffers a profound sense of the very world itself changing as she finds that she must reassess and understand anew large sections of her own life. In such circumstances it is reported that physical things come to feel inconstant and unreliable as past certainties are exposed as false.

17.   This metaphor can be usefully elaborated. Like a web or fabric, a small strain in one place can distort a large section of the pattern: For example, if we were to come to think of people as some kind of program running on a machine there would be consequences for many aspects of our lives and the ways in which events such as death and activities such as studying are meaningful to us.

Conclusion

This essay has now reached a point where we might draw some conclusions. I have analysed what some of the philosophical protagonists of the computer metaphor think. I have given my reasons as to why I think that they are fundamentally mistaken to suppose that representations and processes as they may be said to be present in a computer are in any way analogous to those of the mind. I have followed this with a brief account of the kinds of things that I think are necessary for something to be a person and have made gestures in the direction in which I think this account might be extended and elaborated. I have also provided some indication of where I think functionalism has gone off the rails.

Despite this I feel that I have yet to deal with a fundamental intuition which, though largely unstated, seems to me to underlie most talk about the mind, including the computer metaphor. This intuition gets expressed in many forms, but at its most general it is that any successful account of mind must explain the unitary sense that we all have of being in the world; the sense of the notorious ghost which tends to be required for completeness by most explanations of mental machinery. Sometimes this is glossed over by ill-defined talk about consciousness, sometimes by talk of an 'ego' or 'ego complex' and in many other ways. Dennett expresses this intuition when he says (quoted above page 20), psychology without homunculi is impossible. Many computer metaphor enthusiasts believe that they have evaded this problem by drawing an a analogy between hardware and the brain on the one hand and between mentation or mental process and software on the other. I have noted above (pages 48-49), that this very division not only fails to overcome the problem but seems in fact to be an attempt to smuggle the ghost back in under the name of software.

The positive account that I have given of persons makes no mention of anything which resembles a homunculus or of an 'I' at all. It has concentrated largely on meaning, actions, contexts of actions, and human bodily powers and form. This could appear to deny that there is any such substantial thing which we mean by 'I' and of course I don't want to do that. Therefore I want to conclude this essay with a necessarily brief sketch of an account of this.

In addressing the meaning or significance of 'I' it seems to me illuminating to follow Wittgenstein's oft repeated advice and to look at the context in which we use it. We do not normally talk about the 'I'. When we use the first person singular personal pronoun we are almost always expressing our relationship to something. We say 'I want...', 'I hope...', 'I feel...', 'I own...', 'I believe...', 'I think...', 'I have...', 'I can...', 'I might...', and so on. (This is not simply to remark that most verbs in English can be used in the first person singular present, rather my point is about which verbs are most commonly or frequently used in the first person singular present.) We do not normally say 'My I feels' something, or wants something, or has something. In each of these cases we are expressing something to do with how we stand in relation to the things about which we speak. By saying so we announce, amongst other things, our disposition to act and from this our likely actions may be known. Just what this comes to will vary with the situation: 'I want five brown roles' said appropriately to the shop assistant in the baker's has quite different implications to 'I want fifty thousand pounds' said to a bank teller, while holding a gun, looking menacing, wearing a mask, while in a bank. Both of these suggest different dispositions to 'I want to fly'.

Similarly, the dispositions to act which follow from the use of 'I' in I have a new car', means something quite different to its use in I have a pain in my toe', or I have an appointment at 12.30'. In so far as there is something common to all occasions when we use the first person singular pronoun it is that the relationship and dispositions stated involve our own body. It is significant in this context that the grammar governing 'I' does not allow me to have properties of another person's body. We cannot give a comprehensible literal meaning to 'I have his stomach ache in my right hand', or to I can feel the weight of the rucksack she is carrying on my shoulders'. The use of 'I' indicates, amongst other things, that whatever is being said is relative to the speaker's person. This means not simply his body but his memories, his social contacts and relationships, his dispositions to act and react, his hopes and dreams for the future, and his life.

Personhood then, is not some one quality or thing, let alone some indwelling essence, it is a conglomeration and mishmash of bodily powers, abilities, and history, all of the right kind and of a sufficient complexity to lead us to say that the person has a life. It is the superficial grammar of the way we talk that misleads us into the kinds of analysis that results in us positing ghostly perceivers, thinkers, seers, and the like at the heart of bodily machinery. If we are so misguided as to construe the grammar of I have a pain in my toe' on the model of 'The cat sat on the mat', then we are likely to get into trouble. 'The cat sat on the mat', can be sensibly understood as telling us about the relationship between two named objects, cat' and mat'. If we construe 'I have a pain in my toe', in a similar fashion, as being about the relationship of two named object-like things then we are on a slippery slope to ghosts: Once pain' is thought of as the name of an object-like thing in my body it is natural to ask that 'I' be thought of as the name of an object-like feeler also in my body. The same confusion can easily be ladled out in explanations of seeing, hearing, and so on.

On a wittgensteinian account there is no need for such a ghost. Pain' is not the name of an object-like thing in my body. Pain' is a word which gets its meaning, as does any other word, from the way that it is used in human contexts by language speakers.

This approach seems to beg many questions about personal identity. After all, if there is not something ghost-like in the machine what does personal identity come to? Our bodies, notoriously, change and age.

To me it seems that the answer is that broadly, we, as individual persons, have a grammar. Any particular person will be known to their friends and acquaintances (and enemies) as being the kind of person who would do certain things, would not do other kinds of thing, would say something in a particular way, has a certain appearance, has particular kinds of friends, knows so-and-so, likes this food, comes from a particular background, and so on. These are all the kinds of thing that makes someone to be the kind of person they are, to have, as we say, a particular personality.

All these things are things which may change. Personalities change, develop, and, we hope, mature, over time. People grow up. There is a clear sense in which each of us is not the same person as he or she was ten years ago. It is revealing about our concepts of person and personality that in many contexts we can say, "I am not the same person as I was ten years ago." without fear of being misunderstood or expectation of having to give further explanation in order to be understood. If sufficient of those facts and dispositions which are conceptually connected to our idea of any particular person should change or appear to change, then we would be inclined to say that they are a different person. A crucial part of giving a person a new identity' is giving them a plausible but false history. Disguise, which involves pretending to be someone you are not, is effected by donning atypical clothing, exhibiting a new set of mannerisms, idiosyncrasies, and attitudes, and, sometimes, surgery to change the person's appearance. If someone should undergo a successful sex-change operation, and also change their name, their friends and acquaintances, their style of life, their job, and take on fully their new sexual role, then very little indeed remains to connect them with the person of ten years ago with whom they have bodily continuity.

Despite these possibilities of change, most people display a large measure of personal grammatical continuity over very large portions of their lives. Often these characteristics are established in childhood. Not only do most people remain the same sex all their lives, the habits of thought and typical categories of analysis and basic dispositions to value judgements and much else seem to be set almost permanently in childhood. A child that developed a facility for intellectual thought and perhaps excels in mathematics at school is likely to be disposed to approach problems in most areas throughout his life in a rational and rationalising fashion. A child whose disposition is to understand the world primarily through feeling values such as nice', nasty', emotionally warm', emotionally cold', good', bad', and so on is likely, however much he may learn to rationalise at school, to continue throughout life to judge in this fashion first and to rationalise about it later. It is webs of attitudes of this kind which are conceptually connected to our idea of a particular person, which I want to say form part of their personal identity. In the sense in which this web of features is a grammatical feature of a person, governing how we think and speak of them, personality and personal identity are grammatical features and each person has a unique grammar.

On this view of personhood and personal identity there is no need for a ghost in the machine and in particular no need to think of the human brain as analogous to computer hardware and the mind as analogous to computer software. What we call mind is simply a particular aspect of a living body in the particular social, environmental, linguistic, and historical context of its life. To have a mind is part of what it is for a person to have a life. (Someone who was mindless would have greatly diminished personhood; certainly we expect a person to have a mind.)

To be a person, then, is to be the kind of thing that has such a body, such powers, such abilities, such limitations, such a history, and such attitudes and dispositions, that we will be prone to say that this thing is incarnate and has a life of its own.

Bibliography

Block, N. J. 'Troubles with functionalism' pp. 261-325 in 'Perception and Cognition: Issues in the foundation of psychology', University of Minnesota Press, Minneapolis, Minnesota studies in the philosophy of science, Vol IX, 1978.

Dennett, D. C. 'Content and Consciousness', R.K.P., London, 1969.

Dennett, D. C. 'Brainstorms: Philosophical Essays on Mind and Psychology', Harvester Press, 1979.

Dennett, D. C. 'The Intentional Stance', M.I.T. Press, London, 1987.

Fodor, Jerry. A. 'The Language of Thought', Harvester Press, 1976.

Fodor, Jerry, A. 'Representations: Philosophical Essays on the Foundations of Cognitive Science', Harvester Press, Brighton, 1981.

Goethe, J. W. 'Faust' Part 2, Act 2, Trans. Phillip Wayne, Penguin books, 1949.

Hunt, Earl. 'Cognitive science, Definitions, Status, and Questions', *Annual Review of Psychology, 1989*, Vol. 40 pp. 603-626.

Miender, Terrel. 'The Soul Of The Mark III Beast', pp. 109-113 in *The Mind's Eye: Fantasies and Reflections On self and Soul'*, Douglas Hoffstader and Daniel C. Dennett (Eds.), Harvester Press, Brighton, 1981.

Pollock, John. L. 'How To Build A Person: A Prologomenon', M.I.T.

Press, 'A Bradford Book', 1989.

Putnam, Hilary. 'Minds and Machines', in *Dimensions of Mind*, Sidney Hook (Ed.), Collier Macmillan, 1961.

Putnam, Hilary. 'Language Mind and Reality; Philosophical Papers Vol. 2', Cambridge University Press, 1980.

Putnam, Hilary. 'Computational Psychology and Interpretation Theory', pp 1-17 in *Artificial Intelligence*, *The Case Against*, Rainer Bourn (Ed.), Croom Helm, 1987.

Pylyshyn, Zenon. W. 'Computation and Cognition: Issues in the Foundations of cognitive science', in *The Brain and Behavioural Sciences*, 1980, No. 3, pp. 111-169.

Quine, W. van O. 'Word and Object', M.I.T. Press, Cambridge, Massachusetts, 1960.

Ryle, Gilbert. 'The Concept of Mind', Penguin Books, 1988.

Sayre, Kenneth. Malcolm. 'Recognition: A Study In The Philosophy Of Artificial Intelligence', Notre Dame Press, University of Notre Dame, 1965.

Simons, Geoff. 'Are Computers Alive: Evolution and New Life Forms', Harvester Press, Brighton, 1983.

Weisenbaum, Joseph. 'Computer Power and Human Reason', Penguin Books, 1984.

Wilkes, K. V. 'Functionalism, Psychology, and The Philosophy of Mind', *Philosophical Topics*, Vol. 2, No. 1, pp. 147-167.

Winch, Peter. 'Im Anfang war die Tat', in *Perspectives on Wittgenstein - Papers From The Wittgenstein Colloquium 1976 London Ontario*, Irving Block (Ed.), Blackwell, Oxford, 1981.

Wittgenstein, Ludwig. 'Philosophical Investigations', Trans. G. E. M. Anscombe, Basil Blackwell, 1981.

Wittgenstein, Ludwig. 'On Certainty' Trans. Denis Paul and G. E. M. Anscombe, G. E. M. Anscombe and G. H. von Wright (Eds.), Basil Blackwell, Oxford, 1974.

Wittgenstein, Ludwig. 'Remarks on the Foundations of Mathematics', Trans. G. E. M. Anscombe, G. H. von Wright (Eds.), R. Rhees, and G. E. M. Anscombe, Basil Blackwell, Oxford, 1974.

Wittgenstein, Ludwig. 'Cause and Effect: Intuitive Awareness', in *Philosophia*, Vol. 66, pp. 420.

141